Cambridge Latin Course

Unit 2

FIFTH EDITION

CAMBRIDGE
UNIVERSITY PRESS

CAMBRIDGE
UNIVERSITY PRESS

University Printing House, Cambridge CB2 8BS, United Kingdom

One Liberty Plaza, 20th Floor, New York, NY 10006, USA

477 Williamstown Road, Port Melbourne, VIC 3207, Australia

4843/24, 2nd Floor, Ansari Road, Daryaganj, Delhi – 110002, India

79 Anson Road, #06–04/06, Singapore 079906

Cambridge University Press is part of the University of Cambridge.

It furthers the University's mission by disseminating knowledge in the pursuit of education, learning and research at the highest international levels of excellence.

Information on this title: education.cambridge.org

The Cambridge Latin Course is an outcome of work jointly commissioned by the Cambridge School Classics Project and the Schools Council © Schools Council 1970, 1982 (succeeded by the School Curriculum Development Committee © SCDC Publications 1988).

© University of Cambridge School Classics Project 2001, 2015

First published 1970
Second edition 1982
Third edition 1988
Fourth edition 2001
Fifth edition 2015
Reprinted 2016

Printed in the United States of America

Library of Congress Cataloging in Publication Data

Data available

ISBN 978-1-107-07096-7 Hardback
ISBN 978-1-107-09820-6 Hardback +6 Year Website Access
ISBN 978-1-107-49681-1 Hardback +1 Year Website Access
ISBN 978-1-107-69900-7 Paperback
ISBN 978-1-107-09814-5 Paperback +1 Year Website Access

Cover photograph: front cat © British Museum; background andras_csontos / Shutterstock
Maps and plans by Robert Calow / Eikon
Illustrations by Joy Mellor, Leslie Jones, Peter Kesteven, Neil Sutton, and Lisa Jiang.

Contents

Acknowledgments

The authors and publishers acknowledge the following sources of copyright material and are grateful for the permissions granted. While every effort has been made, it has not always been possible to identify the sources of all the material used, or to trace all copyright holders. If any omissions are brought to our notice, we will be happy to include the appropriate acknowledgments on reprinting.

p. 1, Graham Soffe; pp. 5 *l*, 20 *c*, Cambridge University Museum of Archaeology and Anthropology, accession numbers 1883.766A (p.5) and 1897.225A (p.20); p. 5 *r*, by permission of the National Museum of Wales; pp. 7 *tl*, 21 *bl*, *br*, 22, 31, 35, 37 *t*, *b*, 38 *t*, 41 *2nd from tr*, 57 *b*, 62 *l*, 75, 81 *all* 82 *l*, *c*, 86 *t*, *c*, 89 *l*, 97 *l*, 103 *t*, *b*, 106 *t*, 109 *t*, *br*, 111 *t*, 113, 118 *l*, 119 *third from l*, 128 *c*, *r*, 129 *tr*, 131 *tl*, 133, 141, 143, 144, 145 t, *br*, 146 tr, *cr*, *b*, © The Trustees of the British Museum; p. 7 *bl*, Yorkshire Museums Trust (Yorkshire Museum); pp. 9, 116 *r*, 139 Bardo Museum, Tunis pp. 11, 34, St Albans Museums; pp. 13, 26, 56 *c*, 62 *c*, *r*, © Rheinisches Landesmuseum, Trier, Th. Zühmer; p. 14, detail from Mosaic of Seasons, artifact uncovered in Villa di Dafne, Antioch, Turkey, Roman Civilization, ca 325 / Louvre, Paris, France / De Agostini Picture Library / G. Dagli Orti / Bridgeman Images; p. 18 *t*, Alinari via Getty Images; p. 18 *c*, Lucius Verus Augustus. (130–169). Roman Emperor (161–169). / Photo © Tarker / Bridgeman Images; pp. 18 *b*, 19 *t* CSCP pp. 19 *c*, 37 *c*, *b*, 41 *l*, *tr*, 72 *tr*, 92, 111 *bl*, 125 *r*, 126, 128 *l*, 130, 131 *tr*, 151, Museo Archeologico Nazionale, Naples; p. 20 *t*, Butser Ancient Farm; p. 20 *b*, Institute of Archaeology, University of Oxford; pp. 23, 25, © Museum of London; p. 37 *second from l*, Musei Capitolini, Rome; pp. 38 *b*, 42, Colchester Museums; p. 40 *t*, Dr Simon James; p. 40 *cr*, *br*, pp. 38 *br*, 40 *cr*, *br* by permission of English Heritage (Jim Hancock Collection), © English Heritage; pp. 41 *b*, 59, 68, 69 *t*, *c*, 70, 71 *bl*, *br*, 72 *tl*, *c*, *bl*, *br*, 73 *all*, 74, Fishbourne Roman Palace / Sussex Archaeological Society; p. 54, Bob Croxford / Atmosphere; p. 55 *cl and r*, Museo Archeologico Nazionale, Naples, Italy / The Bridgeman Art Library; p. 56 *t*, Sousse Museum; p. 56 *b*, Classical Numismatic Group Inc.; p. 57 *t*, *c*, © The Colchester Archaeological Trust; p. 58, Dorset County Museum; p. 65, Villa Romana del Casale, Piazza Armerina; p. 67, John Deakin; p. 69 *b*, Adrian Warren / Last Refuge (www.lastrefuge.co.uk); p. 82 *r*, 117 / Don Greenwood; pp. 84–85, *inset*, 88 *tl*, *tr*, Jean-Claude Golvin, *Le Phare d'Alexandrie*, coll. Découvertes Gallimard, © Editions Gallimard Jeunesse; pp. 86 *b*, 88, 91 *all*, Stéphane Compoint; p. 90, IFAO / Alain Leclerc; p. 97 *r*, Vase with painted decoration depicting Europa and the Bull, Roman (glass). / Musee Guimet, Paris, France / Peter Willi / Bridgeman Images; pp. 98, 99, 112, Museo Nazionale Romano, su concessione del Ministero per i Beni e le Attivita Culturali - Soprintendenza Speciale per i Beni Archeologici di Roma; pp. 106 *b*, 107 *t*, *b*, 108 *r*, 109 *bl*, Courtesy of The Corning Museum of Glass, Corning, NY; p. 117, Württemburgisches Landesmuseum, Stuttgart; p. 118 *second from l*, *third from l*, *r*, © RMN-Grand Palais (Musée du Louvre); p. 119 *second from left*, Pushkin Museum, Moscow; p. 119 *r*, The National Gallery, London; p. 122, National Archaeological Museum of Sperlonga; p. 124, Museo Archeologico Nazionale, Naples, Italy / The Bridgeman Art Library; p. 125 *l*, 135 De Agostini / Getty Images; p. 129 *b*, Michael Holford; p. 132, The Metropolitan Museum, New York / Scala; p. 145 *bl* Wolfgang Kachler / Superstock p. 146 *tl*, akg-images / Erich Lessing; p. 148, © RMN-Grand Palais (Musée du Louvre) / Hervé Lewandowski; p. 149 Hypatia of Alexandria, 5th century AD (terracotta) / Ancient Art architecture Collection / Bridgeman Images p. 150, mihtiander/iStock.

All other photography by R.L. Dalladay.

The current edition of the *Cambridge Latin Course* is the result of over forty years of research, classroom testing, feedback, revision, and development. In that period millions of students, tens of thousands of teachers, hundreds of experts in the fields of Classics, history, and education, and dozens of authors have contributed to make the Course the leading approach to reading Latin that it is today.

To list everyone who has played a part in the development of the *Cambridge Latin Course* would be impossible, but we would particularly like to thank individuals and representatives from the following organizations, past and present:

British Museum
British School at Rome
Butser Ancient Farm, England
Castell Henllys, Wales
Council for British Archaeology
Department of Education and Science, London
Fishbourne Palace, England
Herculaneum Conservation Project
Her Majesty's Inspectorate of Schools
North American Cambridge Classics Project
Nuffield Foundation
Qualifications and Curriculum Authority, London
Queen Mary University of London, Department of Classics
Schools Council, London
Southern Universities Joint Board for School Examinations, England
St Matthias College of Education, Bristol
Swedish Pompeii Project
University of Bradford, Department of Classics
University of Cambridge, Faculty of Classics
University of Cambridge, Faculty of Education
University of Cambridge School Classics Project Advisory Panel
University College Cardiff, Classics Department
University College London, Centre for the History of Medicine
University College London, Department of Greek and Latin
University of Leeds, Department of Classics
University of Leeds, School of Education
University of London, Institute of Education
University of Manchester, Department of Art History and Visual Studies
University of Massachusetts at Amherst, Department of Classics
University of Nottingham, Department of Classics
University of Nottingham, School of Education
University of Oxford, Department of Education
University of Oxford, Faculty of Classics
University of Oxford, School of Archaeology
University of Wales, School of Archaeology, History and Anthropology
University of Warwick, Classics Department
Welsh Joint Education Committee

IN BRITANNIA

Stage 13

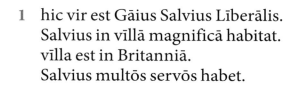

1 hic vir est Gāius Salvius Līberālis.
Salvius in vīllā magnificā habitat.
vīlla est in Britanniā.
Salvius multōs servōs habet.

2 uxor est Rūfilla.
Rūfilla multās ancillās habet.
ancillae in vīllā labōrant.

3 hic servus est Vārica.
Vārica est vīlicus.
vīlicus vīllam et servōs cūrat.

4 hic servus est Philus.
Philus callidus est.
Philus numerāre potest.

5 hic servus est Volūbilis.
Volūbilis coquus optimus est.
Volūbilis cēnam optimam coquere
potest.

6 hic servus est Bregāns.
Bregāns nōn callidus est. Bregāns
numerāre nōn potest.
Bregāns fessus est.
Bregāns dormīre vult.

7 hic servus est Loquāx.
Loquāx vōcem suāvem habet.
Loquāx suāviter cantāre potest.

8 hic servus est Anti-Loquāx.
Anti-Loquāx agilis est.
Anti-Loquāx optimē saltāre potest.
Loquāx et Anti-Loquāx sunt geminī.

9 Salvius multōs servōs habet. servī
labōrant.
servī ignāvī et fessī sunt.
servī labōrāre nōlunt.

trēs servī

trēs servī in vīllā labōrant. haec vīlla est in Britanniā. servī dīligenter labōrant, quod dominum exspectant. servī vītam suam dēplōrant.

Philus: *(pecūniam numerat.)* iterum pluit! semper pluit! nōs sōlem numquam vidēmus. ego ad Ītaliam redīre volō. ego sōlem vidēre volō.

Volūbilis: *(cēnam in culīnā parat.)* ubi est vīnum? nūllum vīnum videō. quis hausit? ego aquam bibere nōn possum! aqua est foeda!

Bregāns: *(pavīmentum lavat.)* ego labōrāre nōlō! fessus sum. multum vīnum bibī. ego dormīre volō.

                (Vārica subitō vīllam intrat. Vārica est vīlicus.)

Vārica: servī! dominus noster īrātus advenit! apud Canticōs servī coniūrātiōnem fēcērunt. dominus est vulnerātus.

Bregāns: nōs dē hāc coniūrātiōne audīre volumus. rem nārrā!

Line numbers: 5, 10, 15

Britanniā: Britannia *Britain*
dēplōrant: dēplōrāre
          complain about
pluit *it is raining*
sōlem: sōl *sun*
Ītaliam: Ītalia *Italy*
redīre volō *I want to return*
aquam: aqua *water*
bibere nōn possum
          I cannot drink
foeda *foul, horrible*
pavīmentum *floor*
lavat: lavāre *wash*
labōrāre nōlō *I do not want*
          to work
fessus *tired*
advenit: advenīre *arrive*
apud Canticōs *among the*
          Cantici (a British tribe)
coniūrātiōnem: coniūrātiō
                plot
vulnerātus *wounded*

Sometimes slaves were kept in chains. Here is a neck chain for slaves which was found in Britain.

A neck chain being worn by volunteers.

coniūrātiō

Vārica rem nārrāvit:

"nōs apud Canticōs erāmus, quod Salvius metallum novum
vīsitābat. hospes erat Pompēius Optātus, vir benignus. in
metallō labōrābant multī servī. quamquam servī multum ferrum
ē terrā effodiēbant, Salvius nōn erat contentus. Salvius servōs ad   5
sē vocāvit et īnspexit. ūnus servus aeger erat. Salvius servum
aegrum ē turbā trāxit et clāmāvit,

"'servus aeger est inūtilis. ego servōs inūtilēs retinēre nōlō.'
postquam hoc dīxit, Salvius carnificibus servum trādidit.
carnificēs eum statim interfēcērunt.   10

"hic servus tamen fīlium habēbat; nōmen erat Alātor. Alātor
patrem suum vindicāre voluit. itaque, ubi cēterī dormiēbant,
Alātor pugiōnem cēpit. postquam custōdēs ēlūsit, cubiculum
intrāvit. in hōc cubiculō Salvius dormiēbat. tum Alātor
dominum nostrum petīvit et vulnerāvit. dominus noster erat   15
perterritus; manūs ad servum extendit et veniam petīvit.
custōdēs tamen sonōs audīvērunt. in cubiculum ruērunt et
Alātōrem interfēcērunt. tum Salvius saeviēbat. statim
Pompēium excitāvit et īrātus clāmāvit,

"'servus mē vulnerāvit! coniūrātiō est! omnēs servī sunt   20
cōnsciī. ego omnibus supplicium poscō.'

"Pompēius, postquam hoc audīvit, erat attonitus.

"'ego omnēs servōs interficere nōn possum. ūnus tē vulnerāvit.
ūnus igitur est nocēns, cēterī innocentēs.'

"'custōdēs nōn sunt innocentēs,' inquit Salvius. 'cum Alātōre   25
coniūrābant.'

"Pompēius invītus cōnsēnsit et carnificibus omnēs custōdēs
trādidit."

metallum *a mine*
hospes *host*
quamquam *although*
ferrum *iron*
effodiēbant: effodere *dig*
ad sē *to him*
inūtilis *useless*
carnificibus: carnifex
        executioner
nōmen *name*
vindicāre voluit
      wanted to avenge
ubi *when*
cēterī *the others*
pugiōnem: pugiō *dagger*
custōdēs: custōs *guard*
ēlūsit: ēlūdere *slip past*
manūs … extendit
     stretched out his hands
veniam petīvit *begged for mercy*
saeviēbat: saevīre *be in a rage*
cōnsciī: cōnscius *accomplice*
supplicium *death penalty*
poscō: poscere *demand*
nocēns *guilty*
innocentēs: innocēns *innocent*
coniūrābant: coniūrāre *plot*
invītus *unwilling, reluctant*

Mining and farming

Metal mining was an important part of the Roman economy, and Britain was a major source of iron, lead, and tin. Many slaves working in the state-operated mines had been sent there as a punishment, and conditions were so bad that this often amounted to a death sentence.

Roman bronze model plowman, with a yoke of oxen.

A lead miner.

However, most of the population continued to work in agriculture. The main crops grown in the province were cereal grains: barley, oats, rye, and especially wheat. As good iron tools and the new heavier plow became available, the yields of grain increased, encouraged by an expanding market. Many of the people working on Salvius' farm would have been local peasants, but he would also have owned some British slaves. Farm slaves were described by one Roman landowner as just "farming equipment with voices," and they lived a harsher life than household slaves.

A large villa like that belonging to Salvius provided much of the industry of the province: market-gardening, fruit-growing, the wool and dye industry, potteries, even the raising of hunting dogs. Such country estates would be supervised by a farm manager. He was sometimes a slave like Varica. The manager was responsible for looking after the buildings and slaves, and for buying food or goods that could not be produced on the villa's own land. Home-grown products such as grain, wool, leather, meat, eggs, timber, and honey could be traded for shellfish, salt, wine, pottery, and ironware.

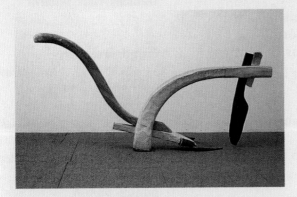

Reconstruction of a Roman plow.

A reconstruction of an early villa in Britain. How many different farming activities can you see?

Bregāns

When you have read this story, answer the questions on page 9.

tum Vārica, postquam hanc rem nārrāvit, clāmāvit,
    "Loquāx! Anti-Loquāx! dominus advenit. vocāte servōs in
āream! ego eōs īnspicere volō."
    servī ad āream celeriter cucurrērunt, quod Salvium timēbant.
servī in ōrdinēs longōs sē īnstrūxērunt. vīlicus per ōrdinēs   5
ambulābat; servōs īnspiciēbat et numerābat. subitō exclāmāvit,
    "ubi sunt ancillae? nūllās ancillās videō."
    "ancillae dominō nostrō cubiculum parant," respondit Loquāx.
    "ubi est Volūbilis noster?" inquit Vārica. "ego Volūbilem vidēre
nōn possum."   10
    "Volūbilis venīre nōn potest, quod cēnam parat," respondit
Anti-Loquāx.
    Bregāns in mediīs servīs stābat; canem ingentem sēcum
habēbat.
    "ecce, Vārica! rēx Cogidubnus dominō nostrō hunc canem   15
mīsit," inquit Bregāns. "canis ferōcissimus est; bēstiās optimē
agitāre potest."
    subitō vīgintī equitēs āream intrāvērunt. prīmus erat Salvius.
postquam ex equō dēscendit, Vāricam salūtāvit.
    "servōs īnspicere volō," inquit Salvius. tum Salvius et Vārica   20
per ōrdinēs ambulābant.
    puerī puellaeque in prīmō ōrdine stābant et dominum suum
salūtābant. cum puerīs stābant geminī.
    "salvē, domine!" inquit Loquāx.
    "salvē, domine!" inquit Anti-Loquāx.   25
    Bregāns, simulac Salvium vīdit, "domine! domine!" clāmāvit.
Salvius servō nihil respondit. Bregāns iterum clāmāvit,
    "Salvī! Salvī! spectā canem!"
Salvius saeviēbat, quod servus erat īnsolēns.
    "servus īnsolentissimus es," inquit Salvius. Bregantem ferōciter   30
pulsāvit. Bregāns ad terram dēcidit. canis statim ex ōrdine
ērūpit, et Salvium petīvit. nōnnūllī servī ex ōrdinibus ērūpērunt
canemque retrāxērunt. Salvius, postquam sē recēpit, gladium
dēstrīnxit.
    "istum canem interficere volō," inquit Salvius.   35
    "illud difficile est," inquit Bregāns. "rēx Cogidubnus, amīcus
tuus, tibi canem dedit."
    "ita vērō, difficile est," respondit Salvius. "sed ego tē pūnīre
possum. illud facile est, quod servus meus es."

in āream
    into the courtyard
in ōrdinēs *in rows*
sē īnstrūxērunt:
    sē īnstruere
        draw oneself up
per ōrdinēs *along the rows*

sēcum *with him*

rēx *king*

equitēs: eques *horseman*
equō: equus *horse*

puerī puellaeque
    the boys and girls
geminī *twins*

simulac *as soon as*

īnsolēns *rude, insolent*

ērūpit: ērumpere
    break away
nōnnūllī *some, several*
retrāxērunt: retrahere
    drag back
sē recēpit: sē recipere
    recover
illud *that*
pūnīre *punish*
facile *easy*

Questions

1 Why did Varica want to inspect the slaves? What did he tell the twins to do (lines 2–3)?
2 In line 4 which two Latin words show that the slaves were in a hurry? Why did they hurry?
3 In lines 8–12 why were the slave girls and Volubilis missing from the inspection?
4 **canem ingentem sēcum habēbat** (lines 13–14). How did Bregans come to have the dog with him? What did he say about the dog (lines 15–17)?
5 Salvius is an important Roman official. How do lines 18–19 show this? Give two details.
6 How did Salvius react in lines 27 and 29 when Bregans called out to him? Why do you think Salvius called Bregans **īnsolentissimus** (line 30)?
7 What happened to Bregans after Salvius hit him?
8 How did the dog nearly cause a disaster (lines 31–32)?
9 Who saved the situation? What did they do?
10 **Salvius … gladium dēstrīnxit** (lines 33–34). What did Salvius want to do? Why did he change his mind?
11 **ego tē pūnīre possum** (lines 38–39). Did Bregans deserve to be punished? Give a reason.
12 What impression of Bregans do you get from this story and why?

Mosaic of a hunting dog.

About the language 1: infinitives

1 Study the following pairs of sentences:

Loquāx cantat.
Loquax is singing.

Loquāx **cantāre** vult.
*Loquax wants **to sing**.*

servī dominum vident.
The slaves see the master.

servī dominum **vidēre** nōlunt.
*The slaves do not want **to see** the master.*

puerī currunt.
The boys are running.

puerī celeriter **currere** possunt.
*The boys are able **to run** quickly.*

Salvius Bregantem pūnit.
Salvius punishes Bregans.

Salvius Bregantem **pūnīre** potest.
*Salvius is able **to punish** Bregans.*

The form of the verb in **boldface** is known as the infinitive. It usually ends in -re and means "to do (something)."

2 Translate the following examples and write down the Latin infinitive in each sentence:

   a Anti-Loquāx currit. Anti-Loquāx currere potest.
   b Bregāns labōrat. Bregāns labōrāre nōn vult.
   c geminī fābulam audīre volunt.
   d senēs festīnāre nōn possunt.

3 Verbs, like nouns, belong to families. Verb families are called conjugations. The vowel that precedes the -re of the infinitive determines the conjugation to which the verb belongs.

For example:

first conjugation	cantāre
second conjugation	vidēre
third conjugation	currere
fourth conjugation	pūnīre

To which conjugation do the following verbs belong?

   a dūcere   **e** festīnāre
   b dormīre   **f** manēre
   c postulāre   **g** audīre
   d habēre   **h** facere

4 The verbs **volō**, **nōlō**, and **possum** are often used with an infinitive. They form their present tense as follows:

(ego)	volō	*I want*		(ego)	nōlō	*I do not want*
(tū)	vīs	*you (singular) want*		(tū)	nōn vīs	*you (singular) do not want*
	vult	*s/he wants*			nōn vult	*s/he does not want*
(nōs)	volumus	*we want*		(nōs)	nōlumus	*we do not want*
(vōs)	vultis	*you (plural) want*		(vōs)	nōn vultis	*you (plural) do not want*
	volunt	*they want*			nōlunt	*they do not want*

(ego)	possum	*I am able*
(tū)	potes	*you (singular) are able*
	potest	*s/he is able*
(nōs)	possumus	*we are able*
(vōs)	potestis	*you (plural) are able*
	possunt	*they are able*

5 **possum**, **potes**, etc. can also be translated as "I can," "you can," etc.:

nōs dormīre nōn possumus.   *We are not able to sleep* or *We cannot sleep.*
ego leōnem interficere possum.   *I am able to kill the lion* or *I can kill the lion.*

6 Further examples:

a ego pugnāre possum.
b nōs effugere nōn possumus.
c tū labōrāre nōn vīs.
d coquus cēnam optimam parāre potest.

e celeriter currere potestis.
f in vīllā manēre nōlō.
g labōrāre nōlunt.
h vīnum bibere volumus.

British hunting dogs were prized all over the Roman world. One is shown here on a Romano-British cup.

Salvius fundum īnspicit

postrīdiē Salvius fundum īnspicere voluit. Vārica igitur eum per
fundum dūxit. vīlicus dominō agrōs et segetem ostendit.

"seges est optima, domine," inquit Vārica. "servī multum
frūmentum in horreum iam intulērunt."

Salvius, postquam agrōs circumspectāvit, Vāricae dīxit,

"ubi sunt arātōrēs et magister? nōnne Cervīx arātōribus
praeest?"

"ita vērō, domine!" respondit Vārica. "sed arātōrēs hodiē nōn
labōrant, quod Cervīx abest. aeger est."

Salvius eī respondit, "quid dīxistī? aeger est? ego servum
aegrum retinēre nōlō."

"sed Cervīx perītissimus est," exclāmāvit vīlicus. "Cervīx sōlus
rem rūsticam cūrāre potest."

"tacē!" inquit Salvius. "eum vēndere volō."

simulatque hoc dīxit, duōs servōs vīdit. servī ad horreum
festīnābant.

"quid faciunt hī servī?" rogāvit Salvius.

"hī servī arātōribus cibum ferunt, domine. placetne tibi?"
respondit Vārica.

"mihi nōn placet!" inquit Salvius. "ego servīs ignāvīs nūllum
cibum dō."

tum dominus et vīlicus ad horreum advēnērunt. prope
horreum Salvius aedificium vīdit. aedificium erat sēmirutum.

"quid est hoc aedificium?" inquit Salvius.

"horreum novum est, domine!" respondit vīlicus. "alterum
iam plēnum est. ego igitur horreum novum aedificāre voluī."

"sed cūr sēmirutum est?" inquit Salvius.

Vārica respondit, "ubi servī horreum aedificābant, domine,
rēs dīra accidit. taurus, animal ferōx, impetum in hoc aedificium
fēcit. mūrōs dēlēvit et servōs terruit."

"quis taurum dūcēbat?" inquit Salvius. "quis erat neglegēns?"

"Bregāns!"

"ēheu!" inquit Salvius. "ego Britannīs nōn crēdō. omnēs
Britannī sunt stultī, sed iste Bregāns est stultior quam cēterī!"

agrōs: ager	*field*
segetem: seges	*crop, harvest*
frūmentum	*grain*
horreum	*barn, granary*
intulērunt: īnferre	*bring in*
arātōrēs: arātor	*plowman*
magister	*foreman*
nōnne?	*surely?*
praeest: praeesse	
	be in charge of
eī	*to him*
perītissimus: perītus	*skillful*
sōlus	*alone, only*
rem rūsticam	*the farming*
cūrāre	*look after, supervise*
simulatque	*as soon as*
hī	*these*
ferunt: ferre	*bring*
ignāvīs: ignāvus	*lazy*
aedificium	*building*
dīra	*dreadful, awful*
taurus	*bull*
impetum: impetus	*attack*
neglegēns	*careless*
Britannīs: Britannī	*Britons*

Line numbers in margin: 5, 10, 15, 20, 25, 30

This wall painting from Roman Gaul shows a master coming to inspect his villa.

About the language 2: -que

1 In this Stage, you have met a new way of saying "and" in Latin:

puerī puellae**que**   *boys and girls*
dominus servī**que**   *master and slaves*

Note that -**que** is added on to the end of the second word.

Rewrite the following examples using -**que** and translate them.

a servī et ancillae
b agricolae et mercātōrēs

2 -**que** can also be used to link sentences together:

dominus ex equō dēscendit vīllam**que** intrāvit.
The master got off his horse and went into the house.

custōdēs in cubiculum ruērunt servum**que** interfēcērunt.
The guards rushed into the bedroom and killed the slave.

3 Further examples:

a Vārica servōs ancillāsque īnspexit.
b Bregāns canisque in ōrdine stābant.
c Salvius āream intrāvit Vāricamque salūtāvit.
d Volūbilis ad culīnam revēnit cibumque parāvit.
e taurus impetum fēcit mūrōsque dēlēvit.

Practicing the language

1 Complete each sentence of this exercise with the most suitable
  infinitive from the box below. Then translate the whole sentence.
  Do not use any infinitive more than once.

īnspicere	dormīre
numerāre	labōrāre
manēre	bibere

  a Philus est callidus. Philus pecūniam . . . . potest.
  b Loquāx et Anti-Loquāx sunt fessī. puerī . . . . volunt.
  c Salvius est dominus. Salvius servōs et fundum . . . . vult.
  d Cervīx est aeger. Cervīx . . . . nōn potest.
  e Volūbilis laetus nōn est. Volūbilis aquam . . . . nōn vult.
  f servī contentī nōn sunt. servī in vīllā . . . . nōlunt.

2 Complete each sentence with the correct form of the noun. Then translate
  the sentence.

  a . . . . in fundō labōrābat. (agricola, agricolae)
  b . . . . fūrem nōn vīdērunt. (custōs, custōdēs)
  c . . . . epistulās longās scrībēbant. (servus, servī)
  d cūr . . . . prope iānuam lātrābat? (canis, canēs)
  e . . . . , quod multam pecūniam habēbat, vīllam magnificam
     aedificāvit. (senex, senēs)
  f . . . . , postquam in forō convēnērunt, ad tabernam contendērunt.
     (amīcus, amīcī)

3 Fill in the gaps in this story with the most suitable verb from the box below, and then translate the whole story. Do not use any word more than once.

cōnspexī	pulsāvī	vituperāvī	obdormīvī	fūgī
cōnspexistī	pulsāvistī	vituperāvistī	obdormīvistī	fūgistī
cōnspexit	pulsāvit	vituperāvit	obdormīvit	fūgit

servus in cubiculō labōrābat. servus, quod erat fessus, in cubiculō
. . . .
    Salvius, postquam cubiculum intrāvit, servum . . . .; statim
fūstem cēpit et servum . . . .
    Rūfilla, quod clāmōrēs audīvit, in cubiculum ruit.   5

Rūfilla: tū es dominus pessimus! cūr tū servum . . . . ?
Salvius: ego servum . . . ., quod in cubiculō dormiēbat.
Rūfilla: heri, tū ancillam meam . . . ., quod neglegēns erat.
            ancilla perterrita erat, et ē vīllā . . . .
Salvius: in vīllā meā ego sum dominus. ego ancillam . . . .,   10
            quod ignāva erat.

Life in the empire

By the time of the eruption of Vesuvius, the city of Rome governed a huge empire. This included lands which we now think of as North Africa, western Europe, the Middle East, and beyond. Although Rome itself had a population of around one million, the number of people who lived in its empire was between 50 and 100 million. Approximately one fifth of the total world population lived in lands controlled by the city.

Rome organized its growing empire into provinces, from Britannia in the north to Aegyptus in the south. Each province was overseen by a Roman governor, assisted by officials such as Salvius, whom you have met in this Stage. These Romans brought with them their friends, relatives, and households, including slaves like Philus and Volubilis from other provinces in the empire.

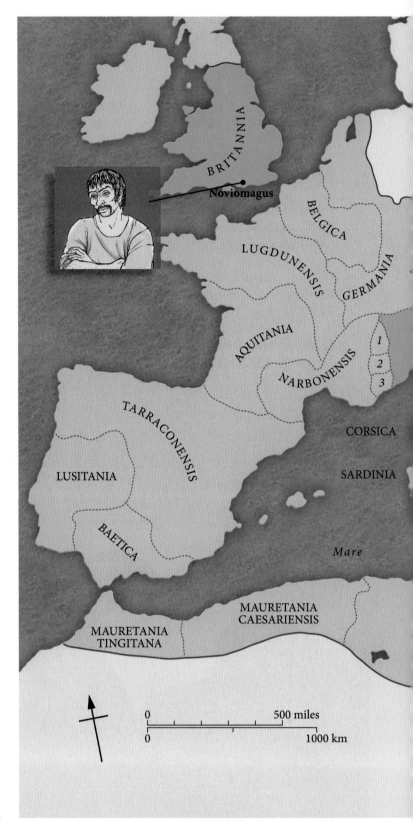

The provinces of the Roman empire in AD 81–82.

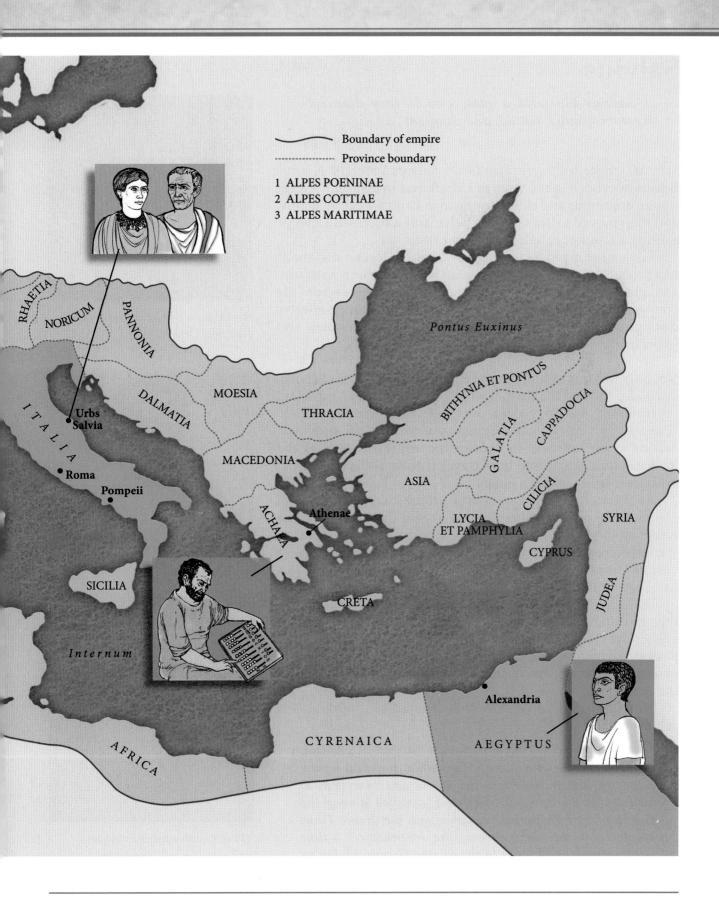

Boundary of empire
Province boundary

1 ALPES POENINAE
2 ALPES COTTIAE
3 ALPES MARITIMAE

RHAETIA
NORICUM
PANNONIA
ITALIA
Urbs
Salvia
Roma
Pompeii
DALMATIA
MOESIA
THRACIA
MACEDONIA
ACHAEA
Athenae
SICILIA
CRETA
Internum
AFRICA
CYRENAICA
Pontus Euxinus
BITHYNIA ET PONTUS
GALATIA
CAPPADOCIA
ASIA
CILICIA
LYCIA
ET PAMPHYLIA
CYPRUS
SYRIA
JUDEA
Alexandria
AEGYPTUS

Salvius

... Salvius Liberalis, a man who is very thorough, organized, quick-witted, and eloquent ...

Pliny

Salvius, whose full name was Gaius Salvius Liberalis Nonius Bassus, was born in the town of Urbs Salvia in central Italy. He was an ambitious and clever young man from a wealthy family, and soon moved to Rome. There he became a successful lawyer, gaining a reputation as an excellent orator.

Salvius belonged to the highest level of Roman society. It was probably the Emperor Vespasian who made him a senator, a sought-after position in Rome. In AD 78 he became one of the youngest members of the Arval Brotherhood, a group of twelve distinguished men who performed religious ceremonies, and in particular prayed for the emperor and his family.

Salvius was put in command of a legion of about 5,000 soldiers. Not only was this military experience a great honor for Salvius, but it also showed the trust in which he was held by Vespasian.

In about AD 80, Salvius was sent to Britannia to help Gnaeus Julius Agricola, the Roman governor of the province. Salvius' main task was to oversee the administration of the justice system. He would have traveled around the province a great deal in his role as a judge.

As Agricola was engaged in a military campaign in the north, it is possible that Salvius would have been given responsibility for running the southern part of the province. We have imagined Salvius and Rufilla living in an impressive villa on the south coast of Britannia, not far from Noviomagus (modern Chichester).

In the stories in this Stage, you have seen Salvius ensuring that farming and mining in the province were carried out efficiently. One of the roles of any province was to provide Rome with income: there would have been significant pressure on men such as Salvius to send as much money as possible to the emperor in Rome.

This inscription, found near his hometown, outlines his achievements:

> **To Gaius Salvius Liberalis Nonius Bassus, ... consul, proconsul of the province of Macedonia, imperial legate, justice of Britain, legate of the 5th Legion Macedonica, member of the Arval Brotherhood, enrolled among the ex-tribunes by the divine Vespasian and the divine Titus, enrolled by the same among the ex-praetors, 4-time quinquennal, and patron of the colony. He was chosen as proconsul of the province of Asia by lot, but excused himself.**

Aerial view of Urbisaglia today (ancient Urbs Salvia).

An Arval Brother.

The inscription dedicated to Salvius. The left-hand edge is missing.

Rufilla

Gaius Salvius Vitellianus set this up in his lifetime to Vitellia Rufilla, daughter of Gaius, wife of Gaius Salvius Liberalis the consul, priestess of the welfare of the emperor, the best of mothers.

The epitaph to Rufilla set up by her son.

The inscription above provides all the information that is known about Rufilla. Her name, Vitellia Rufilla, suggests that she was a member of the gens Vitellia, one of the most influential and important families in Rome. Both Rufilla and Salvius, therefore, were from eminent families. The epitaph was set up by their son, Gaius Salvius Vitellianus; we must wait until a later book to meet him. In accordance with the conventions of epitaphs, he proclaims Rufilla "the best of mothers."

The inscription was found on a gravestone in Urbs Salvia, the hometown of Salvius. Although he and Rufilla spent much of their time in Rome and the provinces, they nevertheless maintained strong connections with Urbs Salvia. It was here that Rufilla was able to reach a public prominence achieved by few Roman women. Doubtless in part the result of the elite position her family and her husband enjoyed, she was honored to become a priestess of Salus Augusta, the goddess who protected the welfare of the emperors. We do not know the details of Rufilla's duties as priestess, but we can be sure that she and Salvius repaid the honor by extensively sponsoring building works and games in Urbs Salvia.

A statue of a Roman priestess.

Although Rufilla's epitaph provides little further information about her, we can speculate about what her life was like when she left Italy to accompany Salvius on his posting to Britannia. She continued to enjoy high social status and likely continued, as far as possible, to maintain the Roman way of life to which she was accustomed. With her exalted position as the wife of the justice of Britain, she would have been in charge of a substantial household, with more slaves and slave girls than were owned by Caecilius and Metella in Pompeii. In our stories, Rufilla has ten slave girls, nine slaves, two hairdressers, and an Egyptian cook.

In Britain, Rufilla probably had a smaller circle of friends around her than Metella enjoyed in Pompeii. She would have socialized largely with the female relatives of Roman administrators and higher-ranking army officers: the wives, daughters, mothers, and sisters who accompanied their menfolk during their service in Britain. Privileged women such as Rufilla may have dedicated a lot of time to writing and dictating letters, and to reading.

The remains of the temple of Salus Augusta in Urbs Salvia.

Britannia

... the spine-chilling sea and the Britons at the very end of the earth.

Catullus

The population of the island is countless. Houses rather like those in Gaul are to be seen everywhere and there are enormous numbers of cattle. They use either bronze or gold coinage.

Julius Caesar

Butser Iron Age Farm.

Although the Romans thought of Britannia as a strange and distant land at the very edge of the known world, the island had its own highly developed cultures before the Romans arrived. We know from archaeological evidence that the Britons, or Celts, were very good metalworkers, carpenters, weavers, and farmers. Copper, and probably tin, were exported to the Mediterranean world long before the arrival of the Romans. The Celts also exported grain, cattle, gold, silver, iron, hides, hunting dogs, and slaves.

Rome, of course, was a city and the Roman concept of civilization was essentially urban-centered. The Celts, however, like many other societies at the time, were tribal, agricultural peoples and lived a primarily rural existence. As a result, Romans writing about the Britons did not usually recognize Celtic achievements.

When the Romans crossed the water to Britain, they came into contact with many separate Celtic tribes. These tribes had certain things in common. They spoke the Celtic language (the basis of Welsh, Irish, and Gaelic today); they used weapons of iron; they were ruled by kings or queens advised by a council of warriors. A chieftain was a wealthy landowner who controlled a small area and owed his loyalty to his monarch. Most chieftains maintained a band of warriors who raided settlements belonging to other tribes and who practiced their fighting skills by hunting wild animals.

Celtic art was characterized by abstract rhythmic patterns, spiral curves, and stylized imaginary animals. Most Celtic art has been found decorating everyday objects made of pottery and various metals.

Roman authors record that Celtic religion was overseen by Druids, powerful priests who acted as judges in disputes. They kept the oral traditions and knowledge of the tribe, and worshipped their gods in sacred woodlands with ceremonies that sometimes included human sacrifice. They encouraged fierce resistance to the Romans, causing them much trouble.

Bronze and enamel ornament from a horse harness, showing the artistry of British craftsmen.

The discovery of coins everywhere indicates that this was no longer a barter economy.

Britain in the first century AD

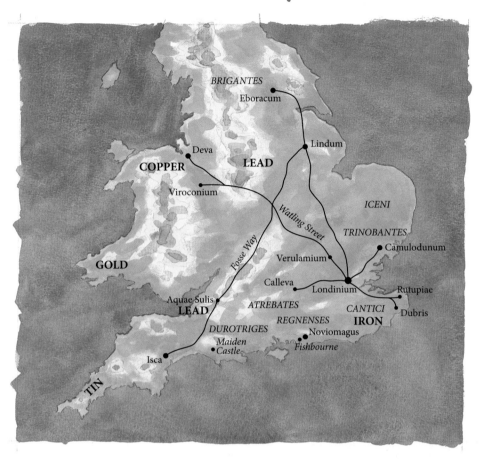

Imports and exports

Among the items exported from Britain in Roman times were grain, hunting dogs, and metals: iron, gold, tin, and lead. In return, Britain imported wine, oil, and other goods from Rome and the rest of the empire.

A pre-Roman British gold coin showing an ear of wheat. CAMV stands for Camulodunum (Colchester) where the coin was minted.

A wealthy Briton who died shortly before the Roman conquest was already importing wine. He had jars of it (amphorae) buried with him.

Vocabulary checklist 13

The way verbs are now listed in the checklists is explained on page 179.

adveniō, advenīre, advēnī	arrive	**ita vērō**	yes
aedificium	building	**nōlō**	I do not want
aeger: aegrum	sick, ill	**novus**	new
alter: alterum	the other, the second	**nūllus**	not any, no
		possum	I can, I am able
cantō, cantāre, cantāvī	sing	**ruō, ruere, ruī**	rush
cēterī	the others, the rest	**sē**	himself
		trahō, trahere, trāxī	drag
custōs	guard	**vīta**	life
dīcō, dīcere, dīxī	say	**volō**	I want
excitō, excitāre, excitāvī	arouse, wake up	**vulnerō, vulnerāre, vulnerāvī**	wound
fessus	tired		
interficiō, interficere, interfēcī	kill		

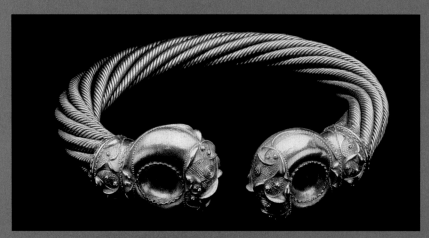

This spectacular gold torque (neck ornament) was made about 70 BC, presumably for a British chieftain.

APUD SALVIUM

Stage 14

1 *multae amphorae sunt in plaustrō.*

Vārica: Phile! portā hanc amphoram in vīllam!

Philus: amphora magna est. difficile est mihi magnam amphoram portāre.

Vārica: cūr?

Philus: quod ego sum senex.

2 *Vārica geminōs in āreā cōnspicit.*

Vārica: Loquāx! Anti-Loquāx! portāte hanc amphoram in vīllam!

Loquāx: amphora gravis est. difficile est nōbīs amphoram gravem portāre.

Vārica: cūr?

Loquāx: quod nōs sumus puerī.

3 *Bregāns prō amphorīs stat.*

Vārica: Bregāns! portā hās amphorās in vīllam!

Bregāns: amphorae gravēs sunt. difficile est mihi amphorās gravēs portāre.

Vārica: sed necesse est!

Bregāns: cūr?

Vārica: necesse est tibi amphorās portāre quod Philus est senex, quod Loquāx et frāter sunt puerī, et …

Bregāns: quod tū es vīlicus!

Rūfilla

Rūfilla in cubiculō sedet. duae ōrnātrīcēs prope eam stant et crīnēs compōnunt. Salvius intrat. Rūfilla, simulatque eum cōnspexit, ōrnātrīcēs ē cubiculō dīmittit.

Rūfilla: Salvī! vir crūdēlis es. ego ad hanc vīllam venīre nōlēbam. in urbe Londiniō manēre volēbam. Londinium est urbs pulcherrima, ubi multās amīcās habeō. difficile est mihi amīcās relinquere.

Salvius: Rūfilla! quam levis es! ubi in urbe Londiniō habitābāmus, cotīdiē ad mē veniēbās. cotīdiē mihi dīcēbās, "ego quoque vīllam rūsticam habēre volō, sed tū mihi nihil dās." tandem vīllam tibi dedī, sed etiam nunc nōn es contenta.

Rūfilla: sed ego vīllam prope urbem habēre volēbam. haec vīlla ab urbe longē abest.

Salvius: tū ipsa eam ēlēgistī. ego, quamquam pretium magnum erat, eam libenter ēmī. nōnne haec vīlla est ēlegāns? nōnne etiam magnifica?

Rūfilla: sed hiems iam appropinquat. nōn commodum est mihi in vīllā rūsticā hiemāre. amīcae meae semper in urbe hiemant. in hōc locō sōla sum. amīcās meās vīsitāre nōn possum.

Salvius: quid dīxistī? sōla es? decem ancillās habēs, novem servōs, duās ōrnātrīcēs, coquum Aegyptium …

Rūfilla: et marītum crūdēlissimum. nihil intellegis! nihil cūrās!
(exit lacrimāns.)

ōrnātrīcēs: ōrnātrīx *hairdresser*
dīmittit: dīmittere
    send away, dismiss

crūdēlis *cruel*
5 Londiniō: Londinium *London*
amīcās: amīca *friend*
relinquere *leave*
levis *changeable, inconsistent*

10 vīllam rūsticam: vīlla rūstica
    a country house
etiam *even*

ab urbe *from the city*
15 tū ipsa *you yourself*
pretium *price*
libenter *gladly*
ēlegāns *tasteful, elegant*
hiems *winter*
20 appropinquat: appropinquāre
    approach
commodum: commodus
    convenient
hiemāre *spend the winter*
25 novem *nine*
lacrimāns *crying, weeping*

A comb and manicure set from Roman London.

A lady with four ōrnātrīcēs.

Domitilla cubiculum parat

I

"Domitilla! Domitilla! ubi es?" clāmāvit Marcia. Marcia anus erat.

   "in hortō sum, Marcia. quid vīs?" respondit Domitilla.

   "necesse est nōbīs cubiculum parāre," inquit Marcia. "domina familiārem ad vīllam invītāvit."

   "ēheu!" inquit Domitilla. "fessa sum, quod diū labōrāvī."   5

   "puella ignāvissima es," inquit Marcia. "domina ipsa mē ad tē mīsit. necesse est tibi cubiculum verrere. necesse est mihi pavīmentum lavāre. curre ad culīnam! quaere scōpās!"

   Domitilla ad culīnam lentē ambulābat. īrāta erat, quod cubiculum verrere nōlēbat.   10

   "ego ōrnātrīx sum," inquit. "nōn decōrum est ōrnātrīcibus cubiculum verrere."

   subitō Domitilla cōnsilium cēpit et ad culīnam quam celerrimē festīnāvit. simulac culīnam intrāvit, lacrimīs sē trādidit.

   Volūbilis attonitus, "mea columba," inquit, "cūr lacrimās?"   15

   "lacrimō quod miserrima sum," ancilla coquō respondit. "per tōtum diem labōrāvī. quam fessa sum! nunc necesse est mihi cubiculum parāre. nōn diūtius labōrāre possum."

anus *old woman*
quid vīs? *what do you want?*
necesse *necessary*
familiārem: familiāris
    relation, relative
diū *for a long time*
domina ipsa
    the mistress herself
verrere *sweep*
scōpās: scōpae *broom*
lentē *slowly*
decōrum: decōrus
    right, proper
lacrimīs sē trādidit
    burst into tears
miserrima *very miserable,*
    very sad
diūtius *any longer*

"mea columba, nōlī lacrimāre!" inquit Volūbilis. "ego tibi cubiculum parāre possum." 20

"Volūbilis! quam benignus es!" susurrāvit ancilla.

coquus cum ancillā ad cubiculum revēnit. dīligenter labōrāvit et cubiculum fēcit pūrum. ancilla laeta

"meum mel!" inquit, "meae dēliciae!" et coquō ōsculum dedit.

coquus ērubēscēns ad culīnam revēnit. 25

nōlī lacrimāre *do not cry*

pūrum: pūrus *clean, spotless*
mel *honey*
ōsculum *kiss*
ērubēscēns *blushing*

II

tum Marcia cubiculum intrāvit. anus vix prōcēdere poterat, quod urnam gravem portābat. Domitilla, ubi Marciam cōnspexit, clāmāvit,

"ecce! dīligenter labōrāvī. cubiculum fēcī pūrum. nunc necesse est tibi pavīmentum lavāre." 5

Marcia, quamquam erat attonita, Domitillae nihil dīxit. sōla pavīmentum lavābat. tandem rem cōnfēcit.

Domitilla statim ad Rūfillam festīnāvit.

"domina," inquit, "cubiculum tibi parāvimus, et pavīmentum fēcimus nitidum." 10

Rūfilla cubiculum cum Domitillā intrāvit et circumspectāvit.

"bene labōrāvistis, ancillae," inquit. "sed, quamquam nitidum est pavīmentum, nōn decōrum est familiārī meō in hōc cubiculō dormīre. nam cubiculum est inēlegāns. necesse est nōbīs id ōrnāre."

"tablīnum est ēlegāns," inquit Domitilla. "in tablīnō, ubi dominus labōrat, sunt multae rēs pretiōsae."

"ita vērō," inquit Rūfilla, "in tablīnō est armārium ēlegantissimum. in tablīnō sunt sella aēnea et candēlābrum aureum. age! Domitilla, necesse est nōbīs ad tablīnum īre." 20

vix *hardly, scarcely*
urnam: urna *jar, jug*
gravem: gravis *heavy*

sōla *alone, on her own*
nitidum: nitidus
     gleaming, brilliant
bene *well*
nam *for*
inēlegāns *unattractive*
id *it*
ōrnāre *decorate*
armārium *chest, cupboard*
aēnea *made of bronze*
candēlābrum *lampstand,*
     candelabrum
aureum: aureus
     golden, made of gold
age! *come on!*
īre *go*

About the language 1: adjectives

1 Study the following sentences:

servus **īrātus** nōn labōrābat.	*The **angry** slave was not working.*
dominus servō **fessō** praemium dedit.	*The master gave a reward to the **tired** slave.*
agricola servum **ignāvum** pūnīvit.	*The farmer punished the **lazy** slave.*

The words in **boldface** are adjectives. They are used to describe nouns. In each of these examples, the adjective is describing the slave.

2 Adjectives change their endings to match the case of the noun they describe.

In the first sentence above, **īrātus** is nominative because it describes a nominative noun (**servus**).
In the second sentence, **fessō** is dative because it describes a dative noun (**servō**).
In the third sentence, **ignāvum** is accusative because it describes an accusative noun (**servum**).

3 Translate the following examples:

  a ancilla perterrita ad culīnam contendit.
  b coquus ancillam perterritam salūtāvit.
  c cīvēs mercātōrem fortem laudāvērunt.
  d cīvēs mercātōrī fortī praemium dedērunt.
  e senex fīlium bonum habēbat.
  f senex fīliō bonō vīllam ēmit.

Write down the Latin noun and adjective pair in each sentence and state whether it is nominative, dative, or accusative.

4 Adjectives also change their endings to match the number (i.e. singular or plural) of the nouns they describe. An adjective is singular if it describes a singular noun, and plural if it describes a plural noun. Compare the following examples with those in paragraph 1:

> servī **irātī** nōn labōrābant.   *The angry slaves were not working.*
> dominus servīs **fessīs** praemium dedit.   *The master gave a reward to the tired slaves.*
> agricola servōs **ignāvōs** pūnīvit.   *The farmer punished the lazy slaves.*

5 Translate the following examples:

  a fēminae laetae per viās ambulābant.
  b fēmina laeta per viās ambulābat.
  c gladiātor leōnēs ferōcēs necāvit.
  d coquus servīs aegrīs cibum parāvit.
  e pictūra pulchra erat in ātriō.
  f Volūbilis ōrnātrīcem trīstem cōnspexit.

Write down the Latin noun and adjective pair in each sentence and state whether the pair is singular or plural.

6 When an adjective changes its ending in this way it is said to *agree*, in case and number, with the noun it describes.

7 Most adjectives come after the noun. However, adjectives like **magnus**, **parvus**, and **multī**, which indicate size or quantity, usually come before the noun they describe. For example:

> Rūfilla multās ancillās habēbat.   *Rufilla had many slave girls.*

Further examples:

  a Bregāns magnum taurum dūcēbat.
  b coquus amīcīs parvam cēnam parāvit.
  c multī Britannī erant servī.
  d agricola parvīs puerīs equum ostendit.

in tablīnō

postrīdiē Salvius et Philus in tablīnō sunt. intrat Rūfilla.

Rūfilla:	mī Salvī!
Salvius:	occupātus sum! necesse est mihi hās epistulās
	dictāre. ego rem celeriter cōnficere volō. ubi est sella
	mea? 5

(Salvius sellam frūstrā quaerit.)

	heus! ubi est ista sella?
Rūfilla:	mī cārissime! aliquid tibi dīcere volō.
Salvius:	tē nunc audīre nōn possum. epistulās dictāre volō.
	ecce! Philus parātus adest. stilī et cērae adsunt – 10
	heus! ubi est armārium meum? quis cēpit?
Rūfilla:	Salvī! audī!

(tandem Salvius uxōrī cēdit et Philum dīmittit.)

Salvius:	ēheu! abī, Phile! nōn commodum est mihi epistulās
	dictāre. 15
Rūfilla:	bene! nunc aliquid tibi dīcere possum. ubi in urbe
	Londiniō nūper eram, familiārem convēnī.
Salvius:	tot familiārēs habēs! eōs numerāre nōn possum.
Rūfilla:	sed hic familiāris est Quīntus Caecilius Iūcundus.
	ubi mōns Vesuvius urbem Pompēiōs dēlēvit, 20
	Quīntus ex urbe effūgit. quam cōmis est! quam
	urbānus!
Salvius:	hercle! ego Pompēiānīs nōn crēdō. paucī probī sunt,
	cēterī mendācēs. ubi in Campāniā mīlitābam, multōs
	Pompēiānōs cognōscēbam. mercātōrēs Pompēiānī 25
	nōs mīlitēs semper dēcipiēbant.
Rūfilla:	stultissimus es! familiāris meus nōn est mercātor.
	Quīntus vir nōbilis est. eum ad vīllam nostram invītāvī.
Salvius:	quid dīxistī? Pompēiānum invītāvistī? ad vīllam
	nostram? 30
Rūfilla:	decōrum est mihi familiārem meum hūc invītāre.
	ancillae familiārī meō cubiculum parāvērunt.
	ancillae, quod cubiculum inēlegāns erat, sellam
	armāriumque tuum in eō posuērunt.
Salvius:	īnsāna es, uxor! Pompēiānī mendāciōrēs sunt quam 35
	Britannī. num tū sellam et armārium ē tablīnō
	extrāxistī?
Rūfilla:	et candēlābrum.
Salvius:	prō dī immortālēs! ō candēlābrum meum! ō mē
	miserum! 40

mī Salvī! *my dear Salvius!*

heus! *hey!*
cārissime *dearest*
aliquid *something*

cēdit: cēdere *give in*

bene! *good!*
nūper *recently*
convēnī: convenīre *meet*
tot *so many*

cōmis *courteous, friendly*
urbānus *smart, fashionable*
paucī *a few*
mīlitābam: mīlitāre *be a soldier*
cognōscēbam: cognōscere
         get to know
mīlitēs: mīles *soldier*

in eō *in it*
num tū . . . extrāxistī?
     surely you did not take?
prō dī immortālēs!
       heavens above!
ō mē miserum!
       oh wretched me!

1 In the first language note in this Stage you met sentences like this:

    cīvis servum **bonum** salūtāvit.   *The citizen greeted the good slave.*

The adjective **bonum** agrees with the noun **servum** in case (accusative) and number (singular). The endings of both words look the same.

2 Now study this sentence:

    cīvis servum **trīstem** salūtāvit.   *The citizen greeted the sad slave.*

The adjective **trīstem** agrees with the noun **servum** in case (accusative) and number (singular) as in the previous example. The endings, however, do not look the same. This is because they belong to different declensions, and have different ways of forming their cases. **trīstis** belongs to the third declension and **servus** belongs to the second declension.

3 Translate the following examples:

  a Quīntus fābulam mīrābilem nārrāvit.
  b in vīllā habitābat senex stultus.
  c gladiātor bēstiās ferōcēs agitābat.
  d dominus amīcō fidēlī dēnāriōs trādidit.
  e multī mercātōrēs vīnum bibēbant.
  f agricola omnibus puerīs pecūniam dedit.

Write down the Latin noun and adjective pair in each sentence and state whether the pair is nominative, dative, or accusative, singular or plural.

A wax tablet with a government stamp on the back. Salvius, as a Roman administrator, may have used official tablets like this one.

Quīntus advēnit

When you have read this story, answer the questions below.

Quīntus ad vīllam advēnit. Salvius ē vīllā contendit et eum salūtāvit.

"mī Quīnte!" inquit. "exspectātissimus es! cubiculum optimum tibi parāvimus."

Salvius Quīntum in tablīnum dūxit, ubi Rūfilla sedēbat. *5*
Rūfilla, postquam familiārem suum salūtāvit, suāviter rīsit.

"cēnam modicam tibi parāvī," inquit. "tibi ostreās parāvī et garum Pompēiānum. post cēnam cubiculum tibi ostendere volō."

Salvius, postquam Quīntus cēnam cōnsūmpsit, dē urbe *10*
Pompēiīs quaerēbat.

"ubi in Campāniā mīlitābam, saepe urbem Pompēiōs vīsitābam. nōnne illa clādēs terribilis erat?"

Rūfilla interpellāvit,

"cūr Quīntum nostrum vexās? nōn decōrum est. difficile est *15*
Quīntō tantam clādem commemorāre."

Rūfilla ad Quīntum sē convertit.

"fortasse, mī Quīnte, fessus es. cubiculum tibi parāvī. cubiculum nōn est ōrnātum. in eō sunt armārium modicum et candēlābrum parvum." *20*

Salvius īrātus nihil dīxit.

Quīntus, postquam cubiculum vīdit, exclāmāvit,

"quam ēlegāns est cubiculum! ego nihil ēlegantius vīdī."

"cōnsentiō," inquit Salvius. "cubiculum tuum ēlegantius est quam tablīnum meum." *25*

exspectātissimus:
    exspectātus *welcome*

modicam *ordinary, little*
ostreās: ostrea *oyster*
garum *sauce*

clādēs *disaster*
terribilis *terrible*
interpellāvit: interpellāre
              interrupt
tantam: tanta *so great, such a*
          great
commemorāre *talk about*
sē convertit: sē convertere *turn*
ōrnātum: ōrnātus
    elaborately furnished,
    decorated
ēlegantius *more tasteful*

Questions

1 Find four examples in this story where Salvius and Rufilla are not telling the truth. In each case explain why their words are untrue.

2 Why do you think Quintus says so little in this story? Think of two reasons.

About the language 3: prepositional phrases

Ablative

1 Study the following examples:

a	Salvius ē **vīllā** contendit.	*Salvius hurried out of the house.*
b	in **tablīnō** est armārium ēlegantissimum.	*In the study there is a very elegant cupboard.*
c	haec vīlla ab **urbe** longē abest.	*This house is far from the city.*
d	Bregāns prō **amphorīs** stat.	*Bregans is standing in front of the amphorae.*
e	nōn decōrum est sine **amīcīs** habitāre.	*It is not right to live without friends.*
f	dē **mercātōribus** audīre nōlō.	*I do not want to hear about the merchants.*

2 The words in **boldface** are nouns in the ablative case. The ablative case is used with certain prepositions in Latin. These include:

ā/ab, cum, dē, ē/ex, in, prō, sine, sub.

3 Compare the nominative singular with the ablative singular and ablative plural in each declension:

	first declension	*second declension*	*third declension*	
nominative singular	puella	servus	mercātor	leō
ablative singular	puellā	servō	mercātōre	leōne
ablative plural	puellīs	servīs	mercātōribus	leōnibus

Accusative

4 Study the following examples:

a	Quīntus ad **vīllam** advēnit.	*Quintus arrived at the house.*
b	ego prope **urbem** habitāre volēbam.	*I wanted to live near the city.*
c	vīlicus per **ōrdinēs** ambulābat.	*The manager was walking through the rows.*
d	Salvius Quīntum in **tablīnum** dūxit.	*Salvius led Quintus into the study.*

The words in **boldface** are in the accusative case. The accusative case is also used with certain prepositions in Latin. These include: **ad, apud, in, per, prope**. What deduction can you make about the preposition **in** when used in Latin?

Oyster shells are common finds on Roman sites in Britain.

tripodes argenteī

tripodes *tripods*
argenteī: argenteus
made of silver

Quīntus in cubiculō sedet. Anti-Loquāx celeriter intrat.

Anti-Loquāx: salvē! necesse est dominō meō ad aulam īre. rēx
Cogidubnus omnēs nōbilēs ad sacrificium
invītāvit.

aulam: aula *palace*

Quīntus: rēgem hodiē vīsitāmus? 5
Anti-Loquāx: ita vērō. quotannīs rēx sacrificium facit, quod
imperātōrem Claudium honōrāre vult.

quotannīs *every year*
imperātōrem: imperātor
emperor

Quīntus: cūr Claudium honōrāre vult?
Anti-Loquāx: decōrum est Cogidubnō Claudium honōrāre.
nam Claudius erat imperātor quī Cogidubnum 10
rēgem fēcit.

honōrāre *honor*

Quīntus: nunc rem intellegō. necesse est mihi dōnum rēgī
ferre. in arcā meā sunt duo tripodes argenteī. illī
tripodes sunt dōnum optimum.

arcā: arca *strongbox, chest*

(Anti-Loquāx ē cubiculō exit et Salviō dē tripodibus 15
*argenteīs nārrat. Salvius statim ad cellārium
contendit.)*

cellārium: cellārius *steward*

Salvius: necesse est mihi rēgem Cogidubnum vīsitāre.
dōnum eī ferre volō.
cellārius: nōn difficile est nōbīs dōnum invenīre, domine. 20
ecce! urna aēnea. antīquissima est. placetne tibi?
Salvius: mihi nōn placet. dōnum aēneum Cogidubnō ferre
nōlō.

(*cellārius Salviō amphoram dēmōnstrat.*)

cellārius: nōnne vīnum est dōnum optimum, domine? 25
Salvius: minimē! Cogidubnus multās amphorās habet, multumque vīnum. rēx vīnum ex Ītaliā cotīdiē importat.

(*subitō Salvius statuam parvam cōnspicit.*)

euge! hanc statuam rēgī ferre possum. aurāta est 30 statua. Quīntus rēgī dōnum argenteum ferre vult; ego tamen aurātum dōnum ferre possum!
cellārius: domine! nōn dēbēs.
Salvius: cūr nōn dēbeō?
cellārius: Cogidubnus ipse tibi illam statuam dedit! 35
Salvius: hercle! necesse est mihi istam urnam ad aulam ferre.

amphoram: amphora *wine jar*
dēmōnstrat: dēmōnstrāre
        point out, show

importat: importāre *import*

aurāta *gilded, gold-plated*

nōn dēbēs *you should not, you must not*

The Celtic chiefs loved Roman silver. This elegant wine cup was made about the time of our story.

Practicing the language

1 Complete each sentence with the correct form of the adjective. Then translate the sentence.

 a servī canem . . . . retrāxērunt.   (ferōx, ferōcem)
 b mercātor . . . . pecūniam āmīsit.   (stultus, stultum)
 c ego . . . . iuvenēs in forō vīdī.   (multī, multōs)
 d ōrnātrīx . . . . coquō ōsculum dedit.   (laeta, laetam)
 e amīcī . . . . lībertum servāvērunt.   (fortēs, fortibus)
 f māter . . . . puerīs cibum parāvit.   (parvī, parvōs, parvīs)
 g Bregāns amphoram . . . . portāre nōlēbat. (gravis, gravem, gravī)
 h domina ancillae . . . . stolam ēmit.   (fidēlis, fidēlem, fidēlī)

2 Complete each sentence with the correct form of the imperfect tense from the list below and then translate. You will have to use one word more than once.

eram	erāmus
erās	erātis
erat	erant

 a vīlicus . . . . anxius; nam Salvius . . . . īrātus.
 b vōs gladiōs habēbātis quod vōs . . . . custōdēs.
 c servī . . . . in āreā, ubi Salvium exspectābant.
 d tū . . . . dominus; decōrum . . . . tibi celeriter prōcēdere.
 e nōs nōn . . . . ignāvī; in fundō dīligenter labōrābāmus.
 f ego in cubiculō iacēbam quod aeger . . . .

Romanization of a province

The first Roman general to lead his soldiers into Britain was Julius Caesar, in 55 BC. Caesar wrote an account of his visit to the island, in which he described the inhabitants as fierce warriors, living on good agricultural or pasture land, in a country rich in timber and minerals.

Caesar returned to the island in 54 BC, this time bringing with him many more troops. He required many Celtic tribes to pay tribute (money) to Rome and to provide hostages. In the southeast of the province Caesar installed Mandubracius as king of the Trinobantes tribe. Mandubracius had appealed to Caesar for help against his rival, Cassivellaunus. Cassivellaunus was forbidden to make any further attack on either Mandubracius or the Trinobantes. When he sailed back to Gaul later that year, Caesar had not conquered Britain, nor did he leave any legions behind, but he had brought Britain into Rome's sphere of political and military influence.

According to the Roman historian Cassius Dio, the Emperor Augustus considered invasions in 34, 27, and 25 BC, but the circumstances were never appropriate, and the relationship between Britain and Rome remained one of trade and diplomacy. The geographer and historian Strabo, writing early in the first century AD, claimed that Rome was able to earn as much from the island by taxing its trade as by conquering it.

In AD 39, the Emperor Caligula assembled a large army on the river Rhine, ready to invade Britain, but it was aborted at the last minute. When the Emperor Claudius successfully invaded in AD 43, almost 100 years after Caesar's first landing, it was on the pretext that he was coming to the aid of the exiled British ruler, Verica of the Atrebates. It is more likely, however, that Claudius needed a military triumph to prove himself as emperor.

Skull of a pre-conquest Briton, who was buried with a crown on his head.

The Romans who conquered: Julius Caesar (above) and the Emperor Claudius (below).

Aulus Plautius' men dug these ditches to defend their camp at Rutupiae (Richborough). The fortress walls were added later, in the third century AD.

Claudius built a triumphal arch at Rome to celebrate the capture of Britain. Part of the inscription survives (left). Claudius also pictured the arch on his coins.

Claudius' campaign was led by the commander Aulus Plautius. Eleven British kings surrendered and Britannia was declared a Roman province, with Aulus Plautius as its first governor. This meant that the Romans were taking over the land as part of their empire. From then on, Roman officials would enforce Roman law. Romans would be able to buy land in the province and use it for agriculture or mining. And the Roman army, fed by an annual tribute in grain and hogs, would be present to keep the peace in the edge-of-empire province, firmly and sometimes brutally.

Our stories in Roman Britain are set during the governorship of Agricola. Agricola stayed in the province for seven years (AD 78–85). He led his army into the Scottish highlands, where he built a number of forts, some of which are still being discovered by aerial photography. His son-in-law, the Roman historian Tacitus, tells us that Agricola effectively put an end to Scottish resistance to Roman rule in AD 84 at the battle of Mons Graupius in Caledonia.

Agricola's mission in the province was not just to secure military victory. According to Tacitus, he also stopped civic corruption and abuses in tax collection. In addition, Agricola "wanted to accustom the Britons to a life of peace, by providing them with the comforts of civilization. He gave personal encouragement and official aid to the building of temples, forums, and houses … He educated the sons of the chiefs … so that instead of hating the Latin language, they were eager to speak it well."

British farmers began to build country villas in the Roman style. Towns, too, built or rebuilt on the Roman grid system, were centered about a forum, with its town hall and law court, and included other public buildings such as public baths, theaters, amphitheaters, and temples. The Romans were tolerant of religions differing from their own, and many Celtic gods were given classical clothing and symbols and assimilated into the Roman pantheon: Apollo-Maponus, Mars-Cocidius, Sulis-Minerva.

This is an artist's reconstruction of the head of a man whose body was found preserved in a peat bog. The Britons may have sacrificed him to their gods, perhaps in an attempt to keep the Romans away.

Roman road (Watling Street) still in use in Britain.

The Romans set up cities in Britain, with forums and temples. This is a model of the temple of the deified Emperor Claudius at Colchester.

Gradually, a network of new roads spread across the province. The roads were originally built for the use of Roman soldiers; but before long they were being extensively used by merchants as well. Trade between the province and the rest of the empire increased rapidly.

Some Britons became very wealthy from trade and welcomed the Romans enthusiastically; many of the leading families responded to Agricola's encouragement to adopt a Roman lifestyle. Other Britons suffered severely from the arrival of the Romans; others again were hardly affected at all. Many no doubt had mixed feelings about becoming part of the Roman empire. It gave them a share in Roman prosperity and the Roman way of life, but it also meant Roman taxes and a Roman governor backed by Roman troops. However they felt, they and their descendants were to be part of the Roman empire for nearly 400 years.

For Romans like Salvius, Rufilla, and Quintus, who found themselves living in a province at the edge of the empire, some aspects of life would have differed greatly from that in Italy. They had to endure different weather, unfamiliar local customs, isolation from friends, and, especially, the lack of urban amenities.

Most inhabitants of Britannia lived in the countryside. A typical small farm belonging to a native Briton would have provided for the basic needs of the farmer, his family, and any slaves, with perhaps a little surplus left over for trade. Their house consisted of a single round room where everyone in the family lived, worked, slept, and ate. There were no windows, and only one low, wide doorway. Light would also have been provided by the open fire in the center of the room which additionally served as a place to cook and as a source of heat. Without a chimney the room must have been quite smoky inside.

A British farmhouse was circular, thereby minimizing heat loss through the walls, which were usually made of wattle and daub attached to a wooden frame. The steeply sloping thatched roof allowed rain and snow to run off quickly.

Wattle and daub: basketwork covered with clay.

The inside of a large roundhouse. There is a coracle (a boat made of animal skins) hanging on the wall and a clay oven in the middle of the floor as well as an open hearth.

About twenty to thirty years after Claudius' campaign in AD 43, simple "villas" began to appear in the countryside. Such a country estate was not a holiday retreat but the center of a working farm community. The majority of the estates discovered in Britain were probably the property not of Romans but of romanized Britons. The villas generally had only four or five rooms, sometimes linked by a corridor; they were built mainly of timber and wattle and daub, with roofs of stone slabs, tiles, or thatch. Some of these early villas are found on the sites of British roundhouses. It is likely that, in the southeast of the province, many Britons were eager to assume the lifestyle of the Romans. Although the owners would have greater privacy and comfort in their new villas, it would have been more difficult and expensive to heat. These early villas are very similar to those found in Roman Gaul and the Britons may have learnt the new building techniques required from Gallic builders and craftsmen.

Later villas were often more complicated in design and were built mostly of stone; the grandest might contain long colonnades, under-floor heating, an ornamental garden, mosaics, and a set of baths complete with tepidarium and caldarium. They also had workshops, barns, living quarters for the farm laborers, and sheds for the animals. In choosing a place to build his villa, the owner would look not only for attractive surroundings but also for practical advantages, such as a nearby supply of running water and shelter from the cold north and east winds.

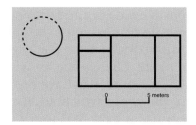

Plan of an early villa built beside a former roundhouse.

Reconstruction of a later villa.

Important events and dates

Emperor	Year	Event
	BC	
	55–54	Julius Caesar's expeditions to Britain.
	44	*Caesar assassinated.*
	34	Invasion of Britain planned.
Augustus	27	*The first emperor*; invasion of Britain planned.
	25	Invasion of Britain planned.
	AD	
Tiberius	14	
Gaius (Caligula)	37	
	39/40	Invasion of Britain collapses.
Claudius	41	
	43	Invasion of Britain takes place under Aulus Plautius.
		Claudius enters Colchester in triumph.
		Vespasian's expedition against the Durotriges.
		Britain becomes a Roman province.
	51	Defeat of Caratacus in Wales.
Nero	54	
	60/61	Revolt of Boudica in East Anglia.
Vespasian	69	*Civil war in Italy.*
	75	The building of Fishbourne palace begins.
	78	Agricola comes to Britain as governor.
Titus	79	*Eruption of Vesuvius.*
	80	Agricola's Scottish campaigns begin.
Domitian	81	Salvius is sent to Britain.
	84	Battle of Mons Graupius.
Honorius	410	Romans cease to defend Britain.

Vocabulary checklist 14

aliquid	*something*	**fidēlis**	*faithful, loyal*
apud	*among, at the house of*	**ipse, ipsa**	*himself, herself*
attonitus	*astonished*	**iste**	*that*
aula	*palace*	**marītus**	*husband*
cotīdiē	*every day*	**necesse**	*necessary*
decōrus	*right, proper*	**num?**	*surely … not?*
dēleō, dēlēre, dēlēvī	*destroy*	**quam**	*how*
		quamquam	*although*
deus	*god*	**-que**	*and*
difficilis	*difficult*	**rēx**	*king*
dīligenter	*carefully*	**ubi**	*when*
domina	*lady (of the house), mistress*		
dōnum	*present, gift*		

Detail of a Roman cavalryman's gravestone. A conquered Briton cowers beneath the horse's hooves.

REX COGIDUBNUS

1 multī Britannī ad aulam vēnērunt.
   senex, quī scēptrum tenēbat, erat rēx
   Cogidubnus.

2 fēmina prope Cogidubnum sedēbat.
   fēmina, quae diadēma gerēbat, erat
   rēgīna.

3 multī Rōmānī Cogidubnō rēs pretiōsās
   dabant. dōnum, quod rēgem valdē
   dēlectāvit, erat equus.

4 duae ancillae ad rēgem vēnērunt.
   vīnum, quod ancillae ferēbant, erat in
   paterā aureā. rēx vīnum lībāvit.

5 servus agnum ad āram dūxit. agnus,
   quem servus dūcēbat, erat victima.

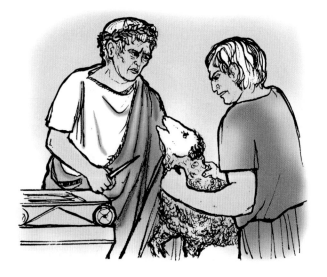

6 sacerdōs victimam īnspexit. victima,
   quam servus tenēbat, bālāvit. sacerdōs
   victimam interfēcit.

ad aulam

*agmen longissimum ad aulam prōcēdēbat. in prīmā parte ībant decem
servī. hī servī, quī virgās longās tenēbant, erant praecursōrēs. in mediō
agmine Salvius et Quīntus equitābant. post eōs ambulābant trēs
ancillae, quae urnam et tripodas portābant. aliae ancillae flōrēs
ferēbant. postrēmō prōcēdēbant vīgintī servī. agmen, quod tōtam viam
complēbat, erat splendidum.*

    *multī quoque Britannī cum uxōribus ad aulam ībant. magna turba
erat in viā. tum Vārica, quī cum praecursōribus equitābat, ad Salvium
rediit.*

Vārica: domine, difficile est nōbīs prōcēdere, quod hī
            Britannī viam complent. ē viā exīre nōlunt. quid
            facere dēbeō?
Salvius: *(īrātus)* necesse est praecursōribus Britannōs ē viā
            ēmovēre. nōn decōrum est Britannīs cīvēs Rōmānōs
            impedīre. ego quam celerrimē īre volō. rēx nōs
            exspectat.

            *(Vārica, quī dominum īrātum timēbat, ad praecursōrēs
            rediit.)*

Vārica: asinī estis! virgās habētis. ēmovēte Britannōs!

*tum praecursōrēs statim virgās vibrābant. multī Britannī in fossās
dēsiluērunt, quod virgās timēbant. duo iuvenēs tamen impavidī in viā
cōnsistēbant. prope iuvenēs erat plaustrum, quod tōtam viam
claudēbat.*

agmen *procession*	
in prīmā parte	
in the forefront	
virgās: virga *rod, stick*	
praecursōrēs: praecursor	
forerunner (sent ahead	
of a procession to clear	
the way)	
equitābant: equitāre *ride*	
flōrēs: flōs *flower*	

facere dēbeō *ought to do*

ēmovēre *move, clear away*
impedīre *delay, hinder*
fossās: fossa *ditch*
dēsiluērunt: dēsilīre
    jump down
impavidī: impavidus
    fearless
cōnsistēbant: cōnsistere
    stand one's ground,
    stand firm
plaustrum *wagon, cart*
claudēbat: claudere *block*

Line numbers: 5, 10, 15, 20

aula

Vārica:	cūr viam clauditis? necesse est dominō meō ad aulam īre. 25
iuvenis prīmus:	nōs quoque ad aulam contendimus. rēgem vīsitāre volumus. sed plaustrum movēre nōn possumus, quod plaustrum rotam frāctam habet.
iuvenis secundus:	amīcus noster, quem nōs exspectāmus, aliam rotam quaerit. amīcum exspectāre dēbēmus. 30

movēre *move*
rotam: rota *wheel*

(Vārica anxius ad Salvium iterum rediit.)

Vārica:	plaustrum, quod vidēs, domine, rotam frāctam habet. difficile est nōbīs prōcēdere, quod hoc plaustrum tōtam viam claudit. 35
Salvius:	*(īrātior quam anteā)* num surdus es? caudex! nōn commodum est mihi in hōc locō manēre. quam celerrimē prōcēdere volō.

anteā *before*
surdus *deaf*

(Vārica ad praecursōrēs iterum rediit.)

Vārica:	caudicēs! ēmovēte hoc plaustrum! dēicite in fossam! 40

dēicite! *throw!*

praecursōrēs, postquam Vāricam audīvērunt, plaustrum in fossam dēiēcērunt. iuvenēs, quī erant attonitī, vehementer resistēbant et cum praecursōribus pugnābant. tum praecursōrēs iuvenēs quoque in fossam dēiēcērunt. Salvius, quī rem spectābat, per viam prōcessit. 45

resistēbant: resistere *resist*

Salvius:	*(cachinnāns)* Britannī sunt molestissimī. semper nōs Rōmānōs vexant.

cachinnāns
laughing, cackling
molestissimī: molestus
troublesome

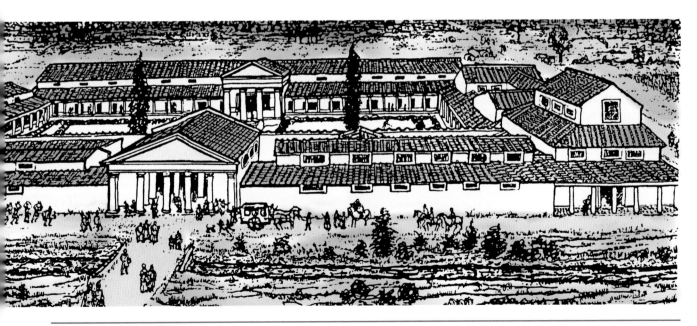

caerimōnia

When you have read this story, answer the questions on page 49.

servus Salvium et Quīntum ad ātrium dūxit. illī, postquam
ātrium intrāvērunt, magnam turbam vīdērunt. multī prīncipēs
Britannicī multaeque fēminae in ātriō erant. sermōnēs inter sē
habēbant. aderant quoque multī Rōmānī, quī prope prīncipēs
sedēbant. haec multitūdō, quae ātrium complēbat, magnum   5
clāmōrem faciēbat.

in mediō ātriō Quīntus et Salvius lectum vīdērunt. in lectō erat
effigiēs cērāta. Quīntus effigiem agnōvit.

"bona est effigiēs!" inquit. "imperātor Claudius est!"

"ita vērō," respondit Salvius. "rēx Cogidubnus Claudium   10
quotannīs honōrat. fabrī ex Ītaliā quotannīs veniunt. fabrī, quī
perītissimī sunt, effigiem faciunt."

subitō turba, quae prope iānuam stābat, ad terram prōcubuit.
prīncipēs Britannicī, quī in mediō ātriō sedēbant, celeriter
surrēxērunt. etiam Rōmānī tacēbant.   15

"rēx adest," susurrāvit Salvius.

per iānuam intrāvit senex. parvus puer senem dūcēbat, quod
claudicābat. rēx et puer lentē per turbam prōcēdēbant. rēx,
postquam ad effigiem advēnit, vīnum lībāvit. tum sacerdōtēs,
quī prope effigiem stābant, victimās ad rēgem dūxērunt.   20
Cogidubnus victimās dīligenter īnspexit. victima, quam rēx
ēlēgit, erat agnus niveus. rēx eum sacrificāvit.

"decōrum est nōbīs Claudium honōrāre," inquit.

sacerdōtēs quoque victimās cēterās sacrificāvērunt. tum
decem prīncipēs Britannicī lectum in umerōs sustulērunt.   25
effigiem ex ātriō portāvērunt. post prīncipēs vēnērunt
sacerdōtēs, quī sollemniter cantābant.

in āreā erat rogus. prīncipēs, quī effigiem portābant, ad rogum
cum magnā dignitāte prōcessērunt. effigiem in rogum
posuērunt. servus rēgī facem trādidit. tum rēx facem in rogum   30
posuit. mox flammae rogum cōnsūmēbant. flammae, quae
effigiem iam tangēbant, cēram liquābant. omnēs effigiem intentē
spectābant. subitō aquila ex effigiē ēvolāvit. omnēs spectātōrēs
plausērunt.

"ecce!" inquit rēx. "deī Claudium arcessunt. animus ad deōs   35
ascendit."

---

caerimōnia *ceremony*

ātrium *hall*
illī *they*
prīncipēs: prīnceps
    chief, chieftain
Britannicī: Britannicus *British*
sermōnēs: sermō *conversation*
inter sē *among themselves,*
    with each other
multitūdō *crowd*
effigiēs cērāta *wax image*
bona *good*
fabrī: faber *craftsman*
prōcubuit: prōcumbere *fall*
claudicābat: claudicāre
    be lame, limp
vīnum lībāvit *poured wine as an*
    offering
sacerdōtēs: sacerdōs *priest*
victimās: victima *victim*
agnus *lamb*
niveus *snow-white*
sacrificāvit: sacrificāre *sacrifice*
umerōs: umerus *shoulder*
sustulērunt: tollere
    raise, lift up
sollemniter cantābant
    were chanting solemnly
rogus *pyre*
cum magnā dignitāte
    with great dignity
facem: fax *torch*
tangēbant: tangere *touch*
liquābant: liquāre *melt*
aquila *eagle*
ēvolāvit: ēvolāre *fly out*
arcessunt: arcessere
    summon, send for
animus *soul, spirit*
ascendit: ascendere *climb, rise*

Questions

1 Where was the crowd gathered for the ceremony? Which three groups of people did Salvius and Quintus see there (lines 2–5)?

2 **haec multitūdō** (line 5). Suggest two English adjectives which you think best describe the crowd in this sentence.

3 Where was the wax image? Whom did it represent (lines 7–9)?

4 **bona est effigiēs**. How did Salvius explain the good quality of the image (lines 11–12)?

5 In lines 13–15, how did the three different sections of the crowd behave?

6 Why was the king accompanied by a boy (lines 17–18)?

7 In lines 18–22, what two offerings did the king make? How did the priests assist the king in this ceremony?

8 After the priests sacrificed their victims, what did the British chieftains do (lines 25–26)?

9 Where was the image placed (lines 28–30)?

10 **servus rēgī facem trādidit**. What did the king do with the torch? What then happened to the image (lines 30–32)?

11 In lines 33–34, why did the spectators applaud?

12 What two things did the king say about Claudius (lines 35–36)? What did the **aquila** represent?

mox flammae rogum cōnsūmēbant.

About the language 1: relative clauses

1   Study the following pair of sentences:

   ancilla urnam portābat.
   The slave girl was carrying the jug.

   ancilla, **quae post Salvium ambulābat**, urnam portābat.
   *The slave girl, **who was walking behind Salvius**, was carrying the jug.*

   The group of words in **boldface** is known as a relative clause, which is
   introduced by a relative pronoun.

2   A relative clause is used to describe a noun. For example:

   vīlicus, **quī cum praecursōribus equitābat**, ad Salvium rediit.
   *The farm manager, **who was riding with the forerunners**, returned to Salvius.*

   prope iuvenēs erat plaustrum, **quod tōtam viam claudēbat**.
   *Near the young men was a wagon, **which was blocking the whole road**.*

   In the first example, the relative clause describes the farm manager; in the
   second, the relative clause describes the wagon.

3   Translate the following examples:

   a   rēx, quī scēptrum tenēbat, in ātriō sedēbat.
   b   vīnum, quod Salvius bibēbat, erat optimum.
   c   ancillae, quae dominum timēbant, ē vīllā festīnāvērunt.
   d   canis, quem Bregāns dūcēbat, ferōcissimus erat.
   e   in viā erant multī Britannī, quī Rōmānōs impediēbant.
   f   cēna, quam Volūbilis parābat, erat splendida.

   For each example, write down the Latin relative clause and the Latin noun it
   describes.

   A complete chart of the relative pronoun, **quī**, can be found on page 167.

lūdī fūnebrēs

I

post caerimōniam rēx Cogidubnus pompam ad lītus dūxit. ibi Britannī lūdōs fūnebrēs celebrāvērunt. aderant Rēgnēnsēs, Canticī, et aliae gentēs Britannicae.

   competītōrēs diū inter sē certābant. Canticī laetissimī erant, quod semper vincēbant. āthlēta Canticus, quī celerrimē cucurrit, cēterōs facile superāvit. alius āthlēta Canticus, quī perītissimus erat, discum longius quam cēterī ēmīsit.

   postrēmō Cogidubnus certāmen nāvāle inter Canticōs et Rēgnēnsēs nūntiāvit. Belimicus nāvī Canticae praeerat; prīnceps Canticus erat, homō superbus et īnsolēns. Dumnorix, quī alterī nāvī praeerat, prīnceps Rēgnēnsis erat, vir fortis et probus. nautae, postquam nāvēs parāvērunt, signum intentē exspectābant. subitō tuba sonuit. nāvēs statim per undās ruērunt. spectātōrēs, quī in lītore stābant, magnōs clāmōrēs sustulērunt.

pompam: pompa *procession*
ad lītus *to the seashore*
gentēs: gēns *tribe*
competītōrēs: competītor *competitor*
5
certābant: certāre *compete*
vincēbant: vincere *be victorious, win*
longius *further*
10
certāmen nāvāle *boat race*
inter Canticōs et Rēgnēnsēs *between the Cantici and the Regnenses*
superbus *arrogant, proud*
15
undās: unda *wave*
in lītore *on the shore*

II

procul in marī erat saxum ingēns. hoc saxum erat mēta. nāvēs ad mētam ruēbant. nāvis Rēgnēnsis, quam Dumnorix dīrigēbat, iam prior erat. Dumnorix, ubi saxō appropinquāvit, nāvem subitō ad dextram vertit.

"ecce!" inquit Dumnorix. "perīculōsum est nōbīs prope saxum 5
nāvigāre, quod scopulus sub undīs latet. necesse est nōbīs scopulum vītāre."

Belimicus tamen, quī scopulum ignōrābat, cursum rēctum tenēbat.

"amīcī," clāmāvit, "nōs vincere possumus, quod Dumnorix ad 10
dextram abiit. hī Rēgnēnsēs sunt timidī; facile est nōbīs vincere, quod nōs sumus fortiōrēs."

nautae Canticī Belimicō crēdēbant. mox nāvem Rēgnēnsem superāvērunt et priōrēs mētae appropinquāvērunt. Belimicus, quī scopulum nōn vīdit, Dumnorigem dērīdēbat. subitō nāvis 15
Cantica in scopulum incurrit. nautae perterritī clāmāvērunt; aqua nāvem complēbat. Belimicus et Canticī nihil facere poterant; nāvis mox summersa erat.

intereā Dumnorix, quī cum summā cūrā nāvigābat, circum mētam nāvem dīrēxit. nāvis ad lītus incolumis pervēnit. multī 20
spectātōrēs Dumnorigem laudāvērunt. Rēgnēnsēs laetī, Canticī miserī erant. tum omnēs ad mare oculōs vertēbant. difficile erat eīs nautās vidēre, quod in undīs natābant. omnēs tamen Belimicum vidēre poterant, quod in summō saxō sedēbat. madidus ad saxum haerēbat et auxilium postulābat. 25

procul	*far off*
in marī	*in the sea*
saxum	*rock*
mēta	*turning point*
dīrigēbat: dīrigere	*steer*
prior	*in front, first*
ad dextram	*to the right*
nāvigāre	*sail*
scopulus	*reef*
sub	*under*
latet: latēre	*lie hidden*
vītāre	*avoid*
ignōrābat	*did not know of*
cursum rēctum	*a straight course*
timidī: timidus	*fearful, frightened*
dērīdēbat: dērīdēre	*mock, make fun of*
incurrit: incurrere	*run onto, collide*
summersa	*sunk*
intereā	*meanwhile*
cum summā cūrā	*with the greatest care*
circum	*around*
incolumis	*safe*
oculōs: oculus	*eye*
eīs	*for them*
natābant: natāre	*swim*
in summō saxō	*on the top of the rock*
madidus	*soaked through*
haerēbat: haerēre	*cling*

About the language 2: imperfect tense of *possum*, etc.

1 In Stage 13, you met the present tense of **possum**, "I am able":

>   Loquāx currere potest.   ego labōrāre nōn possum.
>   *Loquax is able to run.*   *I am not able to work.*

2 You have also met **possum** in the imperfect tense:

>   Loquāx currere poterat.   ego labōrāre nōn poteram.
>   *Loquax was able to run.*   *I wasn't able to work.*
>   or *Loquax could run.*   or *I couldn't work.*

3 The complete imperfect tense of **possum** is:

(ego)	poteram	*I was able* or *I could*
(tū)	poterās	*you (singular) were able*
	poterat	*s/he was able*
(nōs)	poterāmus	*we were able*
(vōs)	poterātis	*you (plural) were able*
	poterant	*they were able*

4 Further examples:

    a servī sōlem vidēre nōn poterant.
    b Bregāns amphoram portāre nōn poterat.
    c nōs labōrāre nōn poterāmus.
    d in urbe manēre nōn poterās.

5 The imperfect tenses of **volō** and **nōlō** are formed in the same way as the imperfect tense of **trahō**: **volēbam**, "I was willing," "I wanted"; **nōlēbam**, "I was unwilling," "I did not want."

6 Translate the following examples:

    a Rūfilla vīllam prope urbem habēre volēbat.
    b nōs redīre nōlēbāmus.
    c servum interficere nōlēbant.
    d cūr festīnāre volēbās?

Practicing the language

1 Complete each sentence with the correct form of the noun and then translate.

    a parvus puer . . . . ad effigiem dūxit. (Cogidubnum, Cogidubnō)
    b ubi sacerdōtēs erant parātī, servī vīnum . . . . dedērunt. (rēgem, rēgī)
    c Cogidubnus, quī prope effigiem stābat, ... ēlēgit. (victimam, victimae)
    d Dumnorix nāvem . . . . ostendit. (amīcōs, amīcīs)
    e facile erat . . . . Belimicum vidēre, quod ad saxum haerēbat. (spectātōrēs, spectātōribus)
    f postquam Dumnorix Belimicum superāvit, rēx . . . . ad aulam invītāvit. (nautās, nautīs)

2 Translate the following sentences:

    a difficile est Cogidubnō festīnāre, quod senex est.
    b spectāculum vidēre nōlumus.
    c necesse est nōbīs fugere.
    d pecūniam reddere dēbēs.
    e Salvius est dominus; decōrum est Salviō servōs pūnīre.
    f commodum est tibi in aulā manēre.
    g victimam sacrificāre vīs?
    h pugnāre nōn dēbēmus!

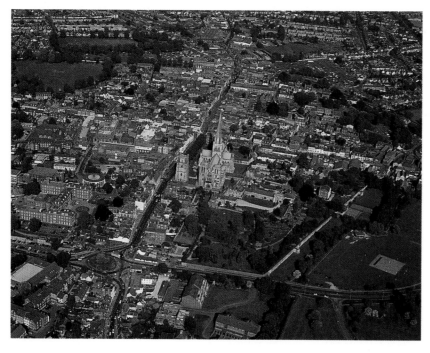

Aerial view of Chichester (ancient Noviomagus). The town walls and the intersecting main streets were laid out in Roman times.

The Celts: friend or foe?

In general the Romans treated the Celtic tribes tolerantly, provided that they fit into the Roman system of law, order, and profitable trade. In fact, the Romans actively encouraged the Britons to take over civil administration in their own regions. Some British rulers, like King Cogidubnus and Queen Cartimandua, chose to co-operate with the Romans and become allies or dependants of Rome. Others, such as Caratacus and Queen Boudica, resisted the Romans bitterly, but unsuccessfully.

Boudica leading her warriors, according to this sculpture in London, England.

Cogidubnus, king of the Regnenses

To Neptune and Minerva, for the welfare of the Divine House, by the authority of Tiberius Claudius Cogidubnus, great king of the Britons, the Guild of Smiths and those in it gave this temple at their own expense. …ens, son of Pudentinus, presented the forecourt.

A slab of stone inscribed with these Latin words was discovered in Chichester not far from the south coast in 1723. When found, the slab was broken, but as soon as the pieces had been fitted together it was clear that this was the dedication stone of a temple built at the request of Cogidubnus in honor of Neptune, god of the sea, and Minerva, goddess of wisdom and craftsmanship. The elegant lettering, carved in the style of the first century AD, suggested the work of Roman craftsmen. Roman dedication stones are rather like the foundation stones which are laid nowadays when an important public building, such as a church, library, or school, is being erected. They state the name of the person or group of people who gave the site

A gold aureus describing the Emperor Claudius as "divine." The horses on the right pull a chariot for a statue of a god, surrounded by figures of victories.

NEPTVNO·ET·MINERVAE
TEMPLVM
PRO·SALVTE·DOMVS·DIVINAE
EX·AVCTORITATE·TI·CLAVD·
COGIDVBNI·REG·MAGNI·BRIT·
COLEGIVM·FABROR·ET·QVI·IN·EO·
SVNT·D·S·D·DONANT·F·AREAM
…ENTE·PVDENTINI·FIL·

A drawing of what remains of the inscription. Some missing letters have been put in according to what is most likely to have been there. The photograph on page 43 shows part of the original stone. You can read the end of Cogidubnus' name. Notice there the neat carving of the well-proportioned letters.

and paid for the building. This particular building was paid for by the local **collēgium** or guild of smiths.

The inscription helps us to construct part of the life story of Cogidubnus himself. Other evidence suggests he was probably a member of the family that ruled the Atrebates. After the Roman invasion in AD 43, the Romans appointed him king of this tribe and the tribe was renamed the Regnenses. Cogidubnus was a faithful supporter of the Romans, and the kingship may have been a reward from the Emperor Claudius for helping them at the time of the invasion. He was granted the privilege of Roman citizenship and allowed to add two of the emperor's names (Tiberius Claudius) to his own. He became a "client king," which meant his relationship with the emperor was one of mutual respect and advantage. He was responsible for collecting the taxes and keeping the peace in his part of Britain. In this way he played an important part in keeping the southern region loyal to Rome, while the legions advanced to conquer the tribes in the north.

By dedicating the new temple to Neptune and Minerva rather than British gods, Cogidubnus publicly declared his loyalty to Rome. The temple was a reminder of Roman power. Its priests may well have been selected from the local British chieftains, many of whom were quick to see the advantages of supporting the new government. And when the inscription goes on to say that the temple was intended "for the welfare of the Divine House," Cogidubnus is suggesting that the emperor himself is related to the gods and should be worshipped. The Romans encouraged the people of their empire to respect and worship the emperor in this way, because it helped to ensure obedience and to build up a sense of unity in a large empire that contained many tribes, many languages, and many religions.

Cartimandua, queen of the Brigantes

Like Cogidubnus, Cartimandua, queen of the Brigantes, openly welcomed the Romans. The Romans were glad to have a buffer between them and the wilder tribes of the far north. Caratacus, a Welsh leader who had been fighting the Romans for seven years, fled to her for refuge. Cartimandua showed her loyalty to Rome by handing Caratacus over to them. In spite of the trouble Caratacus had caused, Claudius, after parading Caratacus and his family in his triumph at Rome, allowed him to live in honorable retirement. For supporting Rome, Cartimandua twice received Roman help in quelling rebellions in her own tribe.

As well as his native Celtic gods, Cogidubnus worshipped Roman ones: (from top) *Neptune and Minerva.*

A silver coin issued by Caratacus, showing the head of Hercules and the letters CARA.

Boudica, queen of the Iceni

The Iceni, a tribe in the east of the province, were at first friendly to Rome. When their king, Prasutagus, died, he made the emperor co-heir, hoping thereby to save his kingdom from harm. The local Roman administrators ignored the will and confiscated all the king's lands and property. Boudica, the wife of King Prasutagus, claimed that when she protested at the injustice, she was flogged and her daughters raped. Boudica and the Iceni would not let these insults go unavenged and, joining with other discontented tribes, they raised a rebellion (AD 60).

At first the rebels were very successful. They met with no effective opposition, since the Roman governor at the time, Suetonius Paulinus, was far away fighting the Druids and their supporters. Boudica's forces looted and destroyed a number of Roman towns, including Londinium (London), and killed many of the inhabitants. Eventually Suetonius Paulinus confronted Boudica and her forces with his legions. Although the Roman troops were heavily outnumbered, their superior training and tactics won them a decisive victory. Rather than face the humiliation of being forced to walk in a triumphal procession as a Roman prisoner of war, Boudica committed suicide by taking poison.

In Roman eyes, Boudica was a remarkable and fearsome figure, not only because she brought them to the brink of disaster, but also because she was a woman who wielded real power. The Britons did not leave a written record of themselves, so evidence for the lives of women is scarce, and comes mainly from archaeology and two Roman writers. From the little we know of their lives, it seems that British women enjoyed higher status than Roman women. Some, like Boudica, from the wealthier families had equal rights with men. They could own property in their own right within marriage, divorce their husbands, and be buried with precious possessions and the same funeral rites as their menfolk. By contrast, even high-born Roman women like Rufilla, although they had an important role to play in running their households, were usually under the legal control of a male relative. No Roman woman ever ruled her people or led them into battle. It is not surprising therefore that Boudica was regarded by the Romans as an unnatural, dangerous, but fascinating woman.

At Colchester, the Iceni massacred some of the inhabitants who had taken refuge in the temple of Claudius. They then burned the city. Archaeologists have found a thick layer of burned debris, including the broken stock of a pottery shop (top) and some charred dates (middle) – both imported goods. The bronze head of Claudius (bottom) was probably wrenched from one of his statues in the city and thrown into a river.

Vocabulary checklist 15

agmen	*column (of people), procession*	**lītus**	*seashore*
		mare	*sea*
alius	*other, another*	**miser**	*miserable, wretched*
aqua	*water*	**nauta**	*sailor*
claudō, claudere, clausī	*shut, block*	**prīnceps**	*chief, chieftain*
commodus	*convenient*	**quī**	*who*
dēbeō, dēbēre, dēbuī	*owe, ought*	**redeō, redīre, rediī**	*return, go back*
equus	*horse*	**sacerdōs**	*priest*
etiam	*even*	**teneō, tenēre, tenuī**	*hold*
impediō, impedīre, impedīvī	*delay, hinder*	**unda**	*wave*
lectus	*couch*	**vincō, vincere, vīcī**	*win*
lentē	*slowly*		

A Roman arrowhead was found in the spine of a Celtic warrior.

IN AULA

Stage 16

1 Cogidubnus Quīntum per aulam
dūcēbat. in aulā erant multae pictūrae,
quās pictor Graecus pīnxerat.

2 rēx iuvenem in hortum dūxit. in hortō
erant multī flōrēs, quōs Cogidubnus ex
Ītaliā importāverat.

3 tum ad ātrium vēnērunt. in mediō
ātriō erat fōns marmoreus, quī aquam
effundēbat.

4 rēx et hospitēs in aulā cēnābant. cēna,
quam coquī Graecī parāverant, optima
erat. servī magnum ōvum in mēnsam
posuērunt.

5 ex ōvō, quod servī in mēnsam
posuerant, appāruit saltātrīx.

6 tum pūmiliōnēs, quōs rēx in Ītaliā
ēmerat, intrāvērunt. pūmiliōnēs pilās
iactābant.

Belimicus ultor

ultor *avenger*

Belimicus, prīnceps Canticus, postquam Dumnorix in certāmine
nāvālī vīcit, rem graviter ferēbat. īrātissimus erat. omnēs
hospitēs, quōs rēx ad aulam invītāverat, eum dērīdēbant. Canticī
quoque eum dērīdēbant et vituperābant. etiam servī, quī dē
naufragiō cognōverant, clam rīdēbant.

    "iste Dumnorix mē dēcēpit," Belimicus sibi dīxit. "mē in
scopulum impulit et praemium iniūstē cēpit. decōrum est mihi
eum pūnīre."

    Belimicus sēcum cōgitāvit et cōnsilium callidum cēpit. erant in
aulā multae bēstiae, quās rēx ē multīs terrīs importāverat. inter
hās bēstiās erat ursa ingēns, quam servus Germānicus
custōdiēbat. Belimicus ad hunc servum adiit.

    "hoc animal est magnificum," inquit. "mē valdē dēlectat. ursam
tractāre volō; eam nōn timeō."

    itaque prīnceps ad ursam cotīdiē veniēbat; ursae cibum et
aquam dabat. paulātim ursam mānsuētam fēcit. tandem sōlus
ursam tractāre potuit.

    mox Cogidubnus cēnam et spectāculum nūntiāvit. amīcōs ad
aulam invītāvit. Belimicus statim ad servum Germānicum
contendit.

    "rēx hodiē spectāculum dat," inquit. "hodiē hanc ursam in
aulam dūcere volō. nunc eam tractāre possum. hospitibus eam
ostendere volō."

    servus invītus cōnsēnsit. Belimicus cachinnāns sibi dīxit,
    "parātus sum. nunc Dumnorigem pūnīre possum."

5

graviter ferēbat *took badly*
dē naufragiō
    about the shipwreck
cognōverant: cognōscere
    find out, get to know
clam *secretly, in private*
impulit: impellere *push, force*
praemium *prize*

10 iniūstē *unfairly*
sēcum *to himself*
ursa *bear*
Germānicus *German*
adiit: adīre *approach,*
    go up to
15 tractāre *handle*
paulātim *gradually*
mānsuētam *tame*

20

25

pūmiliō

ursa

saltātrīx

Salvius et Quīntus prope rēgem recumbēbant.

rēx spectāculum dat

I

rēx cum multīs hospitibus in aulā cēnābat. Salvius et Quīntus prope rēgem recumbēbant. Britannī cibum laudābant, Rōmānī vīnum. omnēs hospitēs rēgī grātiās agēbant.

subitō Belimicus tardus intrāvit.

"ecce! naufragus noster intrat," clāmāvit Dumnorix. "num tū aliam nāvem āmīsistī?"

cēterī Belimicum dērīsērunt et Dumnorigī plausērunt. Belimicus tamen Dumnorigī nihil respondit, sed tacitus cōnsēdit.

rēx hospitibus suīs spectāculum nūntiāvit. statim pūmiliōnēs cum saltātrīcibus intrāvērunt et hospitēs dēlectāvērunt. deinde, ubi rēx eīs signum dedit, omnēs exiērunt. Salvius, quem pūmiliōnēs nōn dēlectāverant, clāmāvit,

"haec cēna est bona. numquam cēnam meliōrem cōnsūmpsī. sed ursam, quae saltat, vidēre volō. illa ursa mē multō magis dēlectat quam pūmiliōnēs et saltātrīcēs."

5

10

15

tardus *late*
naufragus *shipwrecked sailor*

tacitus *silent, in silence*
cōnsēdit: cōnsīdere *sit down*
pūmiliōnēs: pūmiliō *dwarf*
cum saltātrīcibus *with dancing girls*
saltat: saltāre *dance*
multō magis *much more*

II

When you have read this part of the story, answer the questions on page 65.

rēx servīs signum dedit. servus Germānicus, quī hoc signum
exspectābat, statim cum ursā prōcessit et hospitibus eam
ostendit.

    Belimicus, simulatque hoc vīdit, surrēxit, et ad medium
triclīnium contendit.   5

    "mī Dumnorix!" clāmāvit. "facile est tibi iocōs facere. sed ursam
tractāre nōn audēs! ego nōn timeō. ego, quem tū dērīdēs, ursam
tractāre audeō."

    omnēs Belimicum spectābant attonitī. Belimicus, quī servum
iam dīmīserat, ursam ad Dumnorigem dūxit.   10

    "nōnne tū quoque ursam tractāre vīs?" rogāvit īnsolēns. "nōnne
tū hospitibus spectāculum dare vīs?"

    Dumnorix impavidus statim surrēxit et Belimicum dērīsit.

    "facile est mihi," inquit, "hanc ursam superāre. tē quoque,
homuncule, superāre possum."   15

    tum cēterī, quī anteā timuerant, valdē cachinnāvērunt.
Belimicus, ubi cachinnōs audīvit, furēns ursam pulsāvit, et eam
ad Dumnorigem impulit. subitō ursa saeva sē vertit, et
Belimicum ferōciter percussit. tum prīncipēs perterritī clāmōrem
magnum sustulērunt et ad iānuās quam celerrimē cucurrērunt.   20
etiam inter sē pugnābant, quod exīre nōn poterant. ursa, quam
hic clāmor terruerat, ad lectum cucurrit, ubi rēx sedēbat.

    rēx tamen, quod claudicābat, effugere nōn poterat. Dumnorix
in ursam frūstrā sē coniēcit. Salvius immōtus stābat. sed Quīntus
hastam, quam servus Germānicus tenēbat, rapuit. hastam   25
celeriter ēmīsit et bēstiam saevam trānsfīxit. illa dēcidit mortua.

iocōs: iocus *joke*
audēs: audēre *dare*

homuncule: homunculus
                    little man
cachinnāvērunt: cachinnāre
              roar with laughter
cachinnōs: cachinnus
                    laughter
furēns *furious, in a rage*
saeva *savage*
sē vertit: sē vertere
              turn around
coniēcit: conicere
              hurl, throw
immōtus *still, motionless*
hastam: hasta *spear*
trānsfīxit: trānsfīgere
                  pierce

Questions

1 What two things did the German slave do at the king's signal?

2 What boast did Belimicus make (lines 7–8)? How did he show in lines 9–10 that he meant what he said?

3 What two challenges did Belimicus make to Dumnorix (lines 11–12)?

4 Look at lines 14–15. What two things did Dumnorix say that showed he was **impavidus** (line 13)?

5 What two things did Belimicus do when he heard the guests laughing at him (lines 17–18)?

6 What unexpected effect did this have on the bear? Give two details.

7 **perterritī**. How did the chieftains show that they were terrified (lines 19–20)?

8 Why did the guests fight among themselves?

9 Why did the bear run towards the king's couch?

10 Why could the king not escape?

11 In lines 23–26 how did each of the following people react?
   a Dumnorix
   b Salvius
   c Quintus

12 What did their reactions show about each of their characters?

Exotic animals and birds were collected from Africa and Asia, and other parts of the ancient world. Some animals were destined for collections like that held by King Cogidubnus; others ended up being hunted and killed in the amphitheater. This mosaic shows two ostriches being carried up the gangplank of a ship.

About the language: pluperfect tense

1 In this Stage, you have met examples of the **pluperfect** tense. They looked like this:

> in aulā erat ursa ingēns, quam rēx ex Ītaliā **importāverat**.
> *In the palace was a huge bear, which the king **had imported** from Italy.*

> sacerdōtēs, quī ad āram **prōcesserant**, victimās sacrificāvērunt.
> *The priests, who **had advanced** to the altar, sacrificed the victims.*

2 The complete pluperfect tense is as follows:

portāveram	*I had carried*	portāverāmus	*we had carried*
portāverās	*you (singular) had carried*	portāverātis	*you (plural) had carried*
portāverat	*s/he had carried*	portāverant	*they had carried*

3 Further examples:

  a Rūfilla ancillās, quae cubiculum parāverant, laudāvit.
  b in ātriō sedēbant hospitēs, quōs rēx ad aulam invītāverat.
  c agricola nōs laudāvit, quod per tōtum diem labōrāverāmus.
  d Belimicus, quī nāvem āmīserat, īrātissimus erat.
  e Salvius mē pūnīvit, quod ē vīllā fūgeram.

4 Look at the differences between the present, perfect, and pluperfect tenses:

	PRESENT	PERFECT	PLUPERFECT
first conjugation	portat *s/he carries*	portāvit *s/he carried*	portāverat *s/he had carried*
second conjugation	docet *s/he teaches*	docuit *s/he taught*	docuerat *s/he had taught*
third conjugation	trahit *s/he drags*	trāxit *s/he dragged*	trāxerat *s/he had dragged*
fourth conjugation	audit *s/he hears*	audīvit *s/he heard*	audīverat *s/he had heard*

5 Translate these further examples of third conjugation verbs.

  a discēdit   discessit   discesserat
  b scrībit   scrīpsit   scrīpserat
  c facit   fēcit   fēcerat

Quīntus dē sē

postrīdiē Quīntus per hortum cum rēge ambulābat, flōrēsque
variōs spectābat. deinde rēx
    "quō modō," inquit, "ex urbe Pompēiīs effūgistī? paterne et
māter superfuērunt?"
    Quīntus trīstis   *5*
"periit pater," inquit. "māter quoque et soror in urbe periērunt.
ego et ūnus servus superfuimus. ad urbem Neāpolim vix
effūgimus. ibi servum, quī tam fortis et tam fidēlis fuerat,
līberāvī."
    "quid deinde fēcistī?" inquit rēx. "pecūniam habēbās?"   *10*
    "omnēs vīllās, quās pater in Campāniā possēderat, vēndidī. ita
multam pecūniam comparāvī. tum ex Ītaliā discēdere voluī,
quod trīstissimus eram. ego igitur et lībertus meus nāvem
cōnscendimus.
    "prīmō ad Graeciam vēnimus et in urbe Athēnīs habitābāmus.   *15*
haec urbs erat pulcherrima, sed cīvēs turbulentī. multī
philosophī, quī forum cotīdiē frequentābant, contrōversiās inter
sē habēbant.
    "post paucōs mēnsēs, aliās urbēs vidēre voluimus. ad
Aegyptum igitur nāvigāvimus, et mox ad urbem Alexandrīam   *20*
advēnimus."

variōs: varius *different*
quō modō *how*
superfuērunt: superesse
                     survive

Neāpolim: Neāpolis *Naples*
vix *with difficulty*
tam *so*
fuerat *had been*
possēderat: possidēre *possess*
comparāvī: comparāre
                     obtain
cōnscendimus: cōnscendere
       embark on, go on board
prīmō *first*
Athēnīs: Athēnae *Athens*
frequentābant: frequentāre
                     crowd
mēnsēs: mēnsis *month*
Aegyptum: Aegyptus *Egypt*

*The Acropolis (or citadel) of Athens. The prominent building is the Parthenon, the temple of Athena
(whom the Romans called Minerva).*

1 Complete the verb in each relative clause by adding the correct pluperfect ending. Then translate the sentence.

For example: fabrī, quōs imperātor mīs. . . , aulam aedificāvērunt.
fabrī, quōs imperātor **mīserat**, aulam aedificāvērunt.
The craftsmen, whom the emperor had sent, built the palace.

a rēx, quī multōs hospitēs invītāv. . . , eīs cēnam optimam dedit.
b prīncipēs, quī ex ātriō discess. . . , in āream prōcessērunt.
c dōnum, quod ego rēgī ded. . . , pretiōsum erat.
d ancillae, quae ad aulam vēn. . . , hospitēs dēlectāvērunt.
e nōs, quī Belimicum cōnspex. . . , valdē rīsimus.
f tū, quī ursam tractāv. . . , nōn timēbās.

The palace at Fishbourne

When Cogidubnus was made their king, the Regnenses received not only a new leader, but also a new capital town, Noviomagus. It was founded near the south coast, where Chichester now stands. Three miles (five kilometers) to the west is the modern village of Fishbourne, where the remains of a large Roman building were found in 1960 by a workman digging a trench. During the eight years of excavation that followed, the archaeologists discovered that this was no ordinary country house. It was a palace as large and splendid as the fashionable houses in Rome itself, with one set of rooms after another, arranged around a huge courtyard. It is now thought to be one of the largest Roman domestic buildings in northern Europe. No inscription has been found to reveal the owner's name, but the palace was so large, so magnificent, and so near to Noviomagus that Cogidubnus seems a likely owner.

The palace, however, was not the first building erected on the site. Underneath it, the remains of earlier wooden buildings were found, and these go back to the time of the Roman invasion of AD 43, or possibly even before it. One of the wooden buildings was a granary. Pieces of metal and a helmet were also found nearby. These discoveries indicate the presence of soldiers; they may have been the soldiers of the Second Legion, commanded by Vespasian, a brilliant young general who led the attack against the Durotriges, a tribe in the southwest of the province. There was a harbor nearby, where Roman supply ships tied up. It is therefore likely that the Romans first used the site of Fishbourne as a military port and depot where Vespasian assembled his troops,

Model of military store buildings at Fishbourne.

and it is possible that there was a Roman presence at Fishbourne in advance of the campaign of AD 43.

In the years after the soldiers moved on, many improvements were made. The roads were resurfaced, the drainage improved (it was a low-lying, rather marshy site), and the harbor developed. Merchant ships called regularly. A guesthouse was begun and a fine new villa with a set of baths was built in the late 60s.

In about AD 75 a vast area was cleared and leveled, and the villa and baths became part of the southeast corner of a huge new building. Vespasian had become emperor in AD 69: perhaps he was now remembering the loyalty of Cogidubnus and presenting him with the palace in return for his continued support of the Romans. Specialist craftsmen were brought in from Italy: makers of mosaics, marbleworkers, plasterers to make friezes, painters, carpenters, ironsmiths, hydraulic engineers to construct the fountains, and many others. Many traces of the activity of the craftsmen have been found. The floor of the area used by the stonemasons was littered with fragments of marble and colored stone which had been imported from quarries in Italy, the Greek island of Scyros, Asia Minor, and elsewhere. In another area were signs of ironworking where the smiths had manufactured door hinges, handles, and bolts. The craftsmen and the materials were brought in from outside, but all the construction and detailed manufacture were carried out on the site itself, where the builders lived and worked for many years.

The bathhouse (with the white roof) of the original villa was incorporated into the later palace.

As elsewhere in the Roman world, the hypocaust system was used at Fishbourne for heating rooms at the palace.

This aerial view of Fishbourne shows the extent of the palace excavations.

A Roman palace for a British king

The palace at Fishbourne was laid out in four long wings around a central garden.

The north wing contained three suites of rooms arranged around two internal courtyards where important guests could stay.

The hall was possibly used for religious purposes, or for meetings.

Visitors entered the palace through the entrance hall in the middle of the east wing. Some other rooms in this wing may have provided guest accommodations for less important visitors.

The west wing was built on a platform five feet (1.5 meters) higher than the rest of the palace. In the center stood the audience chamber where the king received his subjects and interviewed officials; the other rooms may have been used as offices, or for formal entertaining.

Today the south wing lies under a modern road and houses, but excavations suggest that it may have been the residential suite for King Cogidubnus and his family. Later excavations, undertaken after this model was made, showed that it overlooked a large garden (as large as the main courtyard) leading down to the sea.

The bathhouse in the southeast corner was part of the original villa.

The palace gardens

Like the palace, the garden was planned, laid out, and decorated in the most fashionable Italian style. Whether the owner was Cogidubnus or somebody else, he wished his palace in Britain to be as Roman as possible.

The open area, which measured approximately 100 by 80 yards (90 by 70 meters), was laid out as a formal garden. The two lawns were not rolled and mown like a modern lawn, but the grass was kept short and tidy. Along the edges of the lawns archaeologists have found deep bedding trenches filled with a mixture of loam and crushed chalk where shrubs and flowers such as roses, flowering trees, box, rosemary, lily, and acanthus would probably have been planted.

A line of holes across the eastern side of the garden shows where wooden poles stood to support a trellis for climbing plants. These may have been rambler roses: the Romans were fond of roses and good at growing them.

A broad path, approximately 13 yards (12 meters) wide and surfaced with gravel, ran through the middle of the garden leading from the entrance hall to the audience chamber. Paths ran around the outside of the lawns, and a system of underground pipes brought water to the fountains which stood at intervals along the paths. Small marble and bronze statues would have been placed here and there to provide further decoration.

The reconstruction of the garden at Fishbourne features plants which Cogidubnus might have had in his garden, including the lily and rose.

Box hedges have been planted exactly where the Roman bedding trenches were found.

Elegant walls

The Romans' decorative schemes have been reconstructed from fragments.

One fragment of painted wall plaster from Fishbourne (left) is similar in style to a painting from Stabiae (right).

A frieze made of fine plaster (left) and some of the marble pieces that decorated the walls (right).

Fashionable floors

Above and right: *Cogidubnus' floors were covered with elegant black-and-white mosaics in geometric patterns. Try drawing the different shapes and work out how they fit together.*

This floor, laid by a later owner, had a more complicated pattern. In the center, Cupid rides a dolphin, and legendary sea creatures swim in the semicircular spaces around.

Vocabulary checklist 16

aedificō, aedificāre,
  aedificāvī — *build*

auxilium — *help*

bonus — *good*

cōnsentiō, cōnsentīre,
  cōnsēnsī — *agree*

cōnsilium — *plan, idea*

deinde — *then*

dēlectō, dēlectāre,
  dēlectāvī — *delight*

effugiō, effugere,
  effūgī — *escape*

flōs — *flower*

imperātor — *emperor*

inter — *among*

ita — *in this way*

melior — *better*

nāvigō, nāvigāre,
  nāvigāvī — *sail*

nōnne? — *surely?*

pereō, perīre,
  periī — *die, perish*

pōnō, pōnere,
  posuī — *place, put*

postrīdiē — *(on) the next day*

pūniō, pūnīre,
  pūnīvī — *punish*

simulac, simulatque — *as soon as*

summus — *highest, greatest, top*

tollō, tollere,
  sustulī — *raise, lift up*

vertō, vertere,
  vertī — *turn*

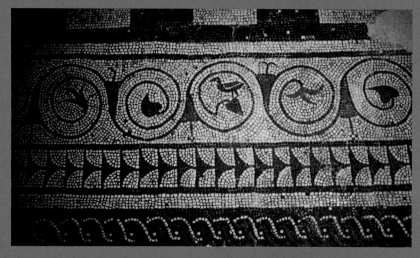

Mosaic tendril border from Fishbourne showing a bird, which probably served as the mosaicist's signature or trademark.

ALEXANDRIA

Stage 17

Quīntus dē Alexandrīā

1 Alexandrīa magnum portum habet.
prope portum est īnsula. facile est
nāvibus ad portum pervenīre, quod in
hāc īnsulā est pharus ingēns. multae
nāvēs in portū Alexandrīae sunt.

2 Alexandrīa est urbs turbulenta. ingēns
turba semper urbem complet. multī
mercātōrēs per viās ambulant. multī
servī per urbem currunt. multī mīlitēs
per viās urbis prōcēdunt. mīlitēs
Rōmānī urbem custōdiunt.

3 postquam ad urbem pervēnimus,
templum vīdimus. ad hoc templum,
quod Augustus Caesar aedificāverat,
festīnāvimus. prō templō Caesaris erat
āra. ego vīnum in āram fūdī.

4 prope hanc urbem habitābat Barbillus,
vir dīves. Barbillus negōtium cum
patre meō saepe agēbat. vīllam
splendidam habēbat. ad vīllam Barbillī
mox pervēnī. facile erat mihi vīllam
invenīre, quod Barbillus erat vir
nōtissimus.

5 Barbillus multōs servōs habēbat, ego
nūllōs.
  "decōrum est tibi servum
Aegyptium habēre," inquit Barbillus.
  inter servōs Barbillī erat puer
Aegyptius. Barbillus, vir benignus,
mihi hunc puerum dedit.

tumultus

I

in vīllā Barbillī diū habitābam. ad urbem cum servō quondam
contendī, quod Clēmentem vīsitāre volēbam. ille tabernam
prope portum Alexandrīae possidēbat. servus, quī mē dūcēbat,
erat puer Aegyptius.

in urbe erat ingēns multitūdō, quae viās complēbat.   5
mercātōrēs per viās ambulābant et negōtium inter sē agēbant.
fēminae et ancillae tabernās frequentābant; tabernāriī fēminīs et
ancillīs stolās ostendēbant. multī servī per viās urbis currēbant.
difficile erat nōbīs per viās ambulāre, quod maxima erat
multitūdō. tandem ad portum Alexandrīae pervēnimus. plūrimī   10
Aegyptiī aderant, sed nūllōs Graecōs vidēre poterāmus. puer,
postquam hoc sēnsit, anxius

"melius est nōbīs," inquit, "ad vīllam Barbillī revenīre. ad
tabernam Clēmentis īre nōn possumus. viae sunt perīculōsae,
quod Aegyptiī īrātī sunt. omnēs Graecī ex hāc parte urbis   15
fūgērunt."

"minimē!" puerō respondī. "quamquam Aegyptiī sunt īrātī, ad
vīllam redīre nōlō. longum iter iam fēcimus. paene ad tabernam
Clēmentis pervēnimus. necesse est nōbīs cautē prōcēdere."

*When you have read this part of the story, answer the questions on
page 79.*

II

itaque ad tabernam Clēmentis contendimus, sed in viā plūrimī
Aegyptiī nōbīs obstābant. in multitūdine Aegyptiōrum erat
senex, quī Graecōs Rōmānōsque vituperābat. omnēs eum intentē
audiēbant.

ubi hoc vīdī, sollicitus eram. puer Aegyptius, quī   5
sollicitūdinem meam sēnserat, mē ad casam proximam dūxit.

"domine, in hāc casā habitat faber, quī Barbillum bene nōvit.
necesse est nōbīs casam intrāre et perīculum vītāre."

faber per fenestram casae forte spectābat. ubi puerum agnōvit,
nōs in casam suam libenter accēpit.   10

postquam casam intrāvimus, susurrāvī,
"quis est hic faber?"
"est Diogenēs, faber Graecus," respondit puer.

---

tumultus *riot*

quondam *one day, once*
ille *he*

tabernāriī: tabernārius
        storekeeper

plūrimī *very many*

sēnsit: sentīre *notice*
melius est *it would be better*

parte: pars *part*

nōbīs obstābant
        *were blocking our way,
        were obstructing us*

sollicitūdinem: sollicitūdō
        anxiety
casam: casa *small house*
nōvit *knows*
perīculum *danger*
fenestram: fenestra *window*
forte *by chance*
accēpit: accipere *take in, receive*

ubi hoc audīvī, magis timēbam. nam in casā virī Graecī eram; extrā iānuam casae Aegyptiī Graecōs vituperābant. subitō servus clāmāvit,

"ēheu! Aegyptiī īnfestī casam oppugnant."

Diogenēs statim ad armārium contendit. in armāriō erant quīnque fūstēs, quōs Diogenēs extrāxit et nōbīs trādidit.

Aegyptiī iānuam effrēgērunt et in casam irrūpērunt. nōs Aegyptiīs fortiter resistēbāmus, sed illī erant multī, nōs paucī. septem Aegyptiī mē circumveniēbant. duōs graviter vulnerāvī, sed cēterī mē superāvērunt. prōcubuī exanimātus. ubi animum recēpī, casam circumspectāvī. fenestrae erant frāctae, casa dīrepta. Diogenēs in mediā casā stābat lacrimāns. prope mē iacēbat puer meus.

"puer mortuus est," inquit Diogenēs. "Aegyptiī eum necāvērunt, quod ille tē dēfendēbat."

15

20

25

magis *more*
extrā iānuam *outside the door*
īnfestī: īnfestus *hostile*
oppugnant: oppugnāre *attack*
effrēgērunt: effringere
                   break down
irrūpērunt: irrumpere *burst in*
septem *seven*
circumveniēbant: circumvenīre
                   surround
animum recēpī: animum
  recipere *recover*
              consciousness
dīrepta *pulled apart, ransacked*
dēfendēbat: dēfendere *defend*

Questions

1 What was the old man doing? What was the crowd's reaction to him (lines 2–4)?
2 **ubi hoc vīdī, sollicitus eram** (line 5). Why do you think Quintus was worried?
3 **puer . . . mē ad casam proximam dūxit** (lines 5–6). Explain why the boy did this (lines 7–8).
4 Why were Quintus and the boy taken into the house (lines 9–10)?
5 **magis timēbam** (line 14). Why was Quintus more frightened now?
6 How had Diogenes prepared for an Egyptian attack on the house? What does this imply about recent events in this part of the city?
7 How did the Egyptians get into the house (line 20)?
8 Why was it difficult to resist the Egyptians (lines 20–21)?
9 Describe the part Quintus played in the fight (lines 22–23).
10 Who was killed? Why do you think he was killed and not anyone else?

About the language: genitive case

1 Study the following sentences:

   ad portum **Alexandrīae** mox pervēnimus.
   *We soon arrived at the harbor **of Alexandria**.*

   in vīllā **Barbillī** erant multī servī.
   *In the house **of Barbillus** were many slaves.*

   mīlitēs Rōmānī per viās **urbis** prōcēdēbant.
   *Roman soldiers were advancing through the streets **of the city**.*

   in multitūdine **Aegyptiōrum** erat senex.
   *In the crowd **of Egyptians** was an old man.*

   The words in **boldface** are in the genitive case.

2 Compare the nominative singular with the genitive singular and genitive plural
   in each declension:

	first declension	*second declension*	*third declension*	
nominative singular	puella	servus	leō	cīvis
genitive singular	puellae	servī	leōnis	cīvis
genitive plural	puellārum	servōrum	leōnum	cīvium

3 Further examples:

   a multī servī in viā clāmābant. Quīntus per multitūdinem
      servōrum contendit.
   b Aegyptiī in casam fabrī ruērunt.
   c nūllī Graecī in illā parte urbis habitābant.
   d fēmina dīves magnum fundum habēbat. multī Aegyptiī in
      fundō fēminae labōrābant.
   e cīvēs viās complēbant. puer Quīntum per turbam cīvium
      dūxit.
   f mercātor togās in tabernā vēndēbat. iuvenēs et puerī ad
      tabernam mercātōris contendērunt.

Egypt, especially Alexandria, had a very mixed population. Many were Greeks like Artemidorus in the portrait on the left; the unnamed man in the center looks Roman. These pictures were found elsewhere in Egypt, but the sculpture of the African man on the right was found in Alexandria itself.

ad templum

per viās urbis quondam cum Barbillō ībam. in multitūdine, quae viās complēbat, Aegyptiōs, Graecōs, Iūdaeōs, Syrōs vīdī. subitō vir quīdam nōbīs appropinquāvit. Barbillus, simulatque eum cōnspexit, magnum gemitum dedit.

Barbillus:	ēheu! quam miserī sumus! ecce Plancus, vir doctissimus, quī numquam tacet! semper dē templīs deōrum et dē aliīs monumentīs garrīre vult.
Plancus:	salvē, mī dulcissime! quid hodiē agis? quō contendis?
Barbillus:	(*invītus*) ad templum.
Plancus:	ad templum Augustī?
Barbillus:	minimē, ad templum Serāpidis īmus. nunc festīnāre dēbēmus, quod iter longum est. nōnne tū negōtium cum aliīs mercātōribus agere dēbēs? valē!
Plancus:	hodiē ōtiōsus sum. commodum est mihi ad templum Serāpidis īre. dē Serāpide vōbīs nārrāre possum.

(Plancus nōbīscum ībat garriēns. nōbīs dē omnibus monumentīs nārrāre coepit.)

Barbillus:	(*susurrāns*) amīcus noster loquācior est quam psittacus et obstinātior quam asinus.

Iūdaeōs: Iūdaeī *Jews*
Syrōs: Syrī *Syrians*
vir quīdam *a certain man, someone*
5 **gemitum: gemitus** *groan*
doctissimus: doctus *learned, clever*
monumentīs: monumentum *monument*
10 **garrīre** *chatter, gossip*
mī dulcissime *my very dear friend*
quid . . . agis? *how are you?*

15

garriēns *chattering*
coepit *began*
susurrāns *whispering*
loquācior: loquāx *talkative*
20 **psittacus** *parrot*
obstinātior: obstinātus *obstinate, stubborn*

Plancus:	nunc ad templum Serāpidis advēnimus. spectāte templum! quam magnificum! spectāte cellam! statuam vīdistis, quae in cellā est? deus ibi cum magnā dignitāte sedet. in capite deī est canistrum. Serāpis enim est deus quī segetēs cūrat. opportūnē 25 hūc vēnimus. hōra quārta est. nunc sacerdōtēs in ārā sacrificium facere solent.

(subitō tuba sonuit. sacerdōtēs ē cellā templī ad āram prōcessērunt.)

sacerdōs:	tacēte vōs omnēs, quī adestis! tacēte vōs, quī hoc 30 sacrificium vidēre vultis!

(omnēs virī fēminaeque statim tacuērunt.)

Barbillus:	*(rīdēns et susurrāns)* ehem! vidēsne Plancum? ubi sacerdōs silentium poposcit, etiam ille dēnique tacuit. mīrāculum est. deus nōs servāvit. 35

cellam: cella *sanctuary*

in capite *on the head*
canistrum *basket*
enim *for*
opportūnē *just at the right time*
hōra *hour*
quārta *fourth*
ārā: āra *altar*
facere solent *are accustomed to making, usually make*

rīdēns *laughing, smiling*
ehem! *well, well!*
silentium *silence*
dēnique *at last, finally*
mīrāculum *miracle*

Portrait of a priest of Serapis.

This sphinx marks the site of the temple of Serapis.

Left: *The god Serapis, with the corn measure on his head.*

Practicing the language

1 Complete each sentence with the correct form of the noun and then translate.

    a in multitūdine . . . . stābat senex. (Aegyptiōrum, Aegyptiī)
    b faber per fenestram . . . . spectābat. (casārum, casae)
    c in viīs . . . . erant multī mercātōrēs. (urbis, urbium)
    d domina per turbam . . . . festīnāvit. (ancillae, ancillārum)
    e nōs ad templum Serāpidis pervēnimus. prō templō . . . . stābant multī cīvēs. (deī, deōrum)
    f mercātōrēs vīllās splendidās habēbant. in vīllīs . . . . erant statuae pretiōsae. (mercātōris, mercātōrum)

2 Complete each sentence with the correct form of the verb and then translate.

    a ubi Diogenēs hoc dīxit, nōs casam . . . . (intrāvī, intrāvimus)
    b Aegyptiī tabernam oppugnāvērunt, ubi vōs templum . . . . (vīsitābās, vīsitābātis)
    c ego, ubi in urbe eram, tēcum negōtium . . . . (agēbam, agēbāmus)
    d tū senem, quī Rōmānōs vituperābat, ... (audīvistī, audīvistis)
    e nōs . . . ., quod sacerdōtēs ad āram prōcēdēbant. (tacēbāmus, tacēbam)
    f vōs auxilium mihi semper . . . . (dabātis, dabās)
    g pestis es! togās sordidās mihi . . . . (vēndidistis, vēndidistī)
    h ad portum ambulābam. multōs mīlitēs Rōmānōs . . . . (vīdī, vīdimus)

3 Complete each sentence with the correct verb from the box below and then translate.

volō	volumus	possum	possumus
vīs	vultis	potes	potestis
vult	volunt	potest	possunt

    a māne ad portum ambulāre soleō, quod nāvēs spectāre . . . .
    b mihi valdē placet puellam audīre, quae suāviter cantāre . . . .
    c Barbille! nōnne dē monumentīs audīre . . . . ?
    d iter longum iam fēcistis; ad vīllam hodiē pervenīre nōn . . . .
    e multī virī fēminaeque ad templum contendunt, quod sacrificium vidēre . . . .
    f paucī sumus. Aegyptiōs superāre nōn . . . .
    g māter, quae fīliō dōnum dare . . . ., togās in tabernā īnspicit.
    h Aegyptiī fūstēs habent; Graecī eīs resistere nōn . . . .

Alexandria

Alexandria had three harbors. The Great Harbor and the Western Harbor lay on either side of a breakwater three-quarters of a mile (1.2 kilometers) long which joined Pharos island to the mainland. The third harbor was on the large lake which lay behind the city and was connected by canals to the river Nile. From here goods were brought by a further canal, or overland, to the Red Sea; this was the route that led to India.

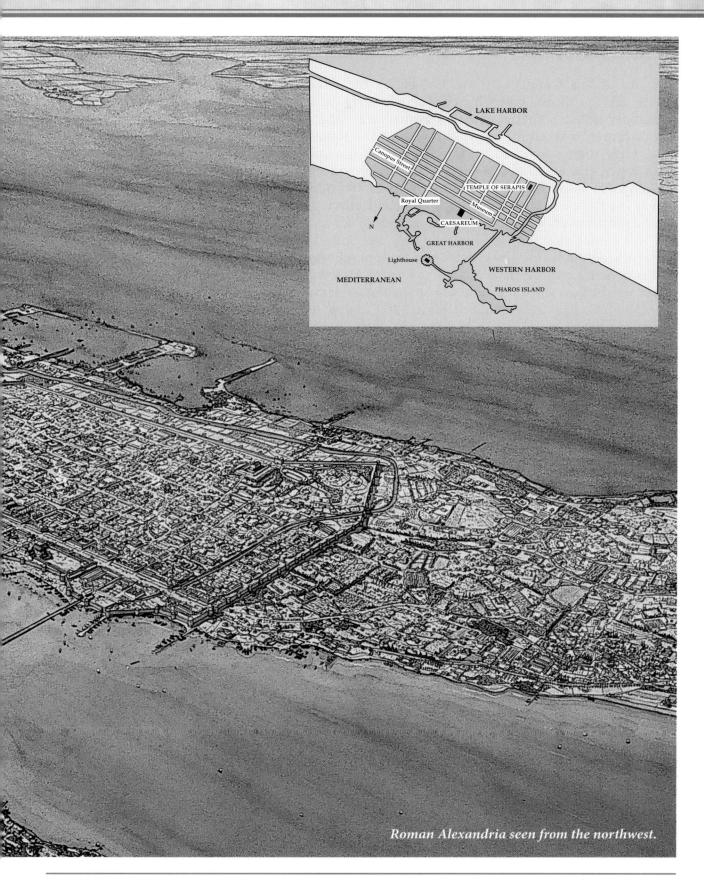

Map labels:

LAKE HARBOR

Canopus Street

TEMPLE OF SERAPIS

Royal Quarter

Museum

CAESAREUM

GREAT HARBOR

N

Lighthouse

MEDITERRANEAN

WESTERN HARBOR

PHAROS ISLAND

Roman Alexandria seen from the northwest.

Alexandria

The site of this famous city was chosen by the Greek king, Alexander the Great, when he conquered Egypt in 331 BC. Alexander noted both the excellent agricultural land and the fine harbor of a small fishing village west of the mouth of the Nile. Here there was good anchorage, a healthy climate and fresh water, and limestone quarries nearby to provide stone for building. He commanded his architect to plan and build a city which was to be a new center of trade and civilization.

Alexander died while the city was still developing, but the city was named after him and his body was later buried there in a magnificent tomb. He was succeeded as ruler by Ptolemy, one of his generals, whose descendants governed Alexandria and Egypt for the next three hundred years. The last Ptolemaic ruler was Queen Cleopatra. With her defeat in 30 BC, Egypt became a Roman province.

Alexander the Great.

By the first century AD, Alexandria was probably as large and splendid as Rome itself; it was certainly the greatest city in the eastern part of the empire, with perhaps a million inhabitants. Much of its wealth and importance was due to its position. It stood at a meeting place of great trade routes and was therefore excellently placed for trading on a large scale. Merchants and businessmen were attracted to the city because it offered them safe harbors for their ships, a large number of dockworkers to handle their cargoes, huge warehouses for storage, and a busy market for buying and selling.

Coin of Alexandria, showing a ship passing the lighthouse.

Into Alexandria came luxury goods such as bronze statues from Greece or fine Italian wines, and raw materials such as wood and marble to be used by craftsmen in the local workshops. Out to other countries went wheat in enormous quantities, papyrus, glassware, and much else. A list in the *Red Sea Guide Book*, written by an Alexandrian merchant in the first century AD, gives some idea of the vast range of goods bought and sold in the city: "clothes, cotton, skins, muslins, silks, brass, copper, iron, gold, silver, silver plate, tin, axes, adzes, glass, ivory, tortoise shell, rhinoceros horn, wine, olive oil, sesame oil, rice, butter, honey, wheat, myrrh, frankincense, cinnamon, fragrant gums, papyrus."

The Great Harbor in Alexandria today.

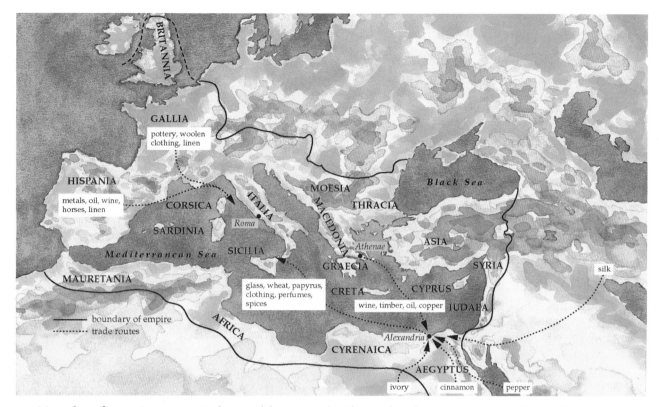

Map labels: BRITANNIA, GALLIA, pottery, woolen clothing, linen, HISPANIA, metals, oil, wine, horses, linen, CORSICA, ITALIA, SARDINIA, Roma, Mediterranean Sea, SICILIA, MOESIA, THRACIA, Black Sea, MACEDONIA, ASIA, Athenae, GRAECIA, SYRIA, silk, MAURETANIA, glass, wheat, papyrus, clothing, perfumes, spices, CRETA, CYPRUS, wine, timber, oil, copper, IUDAEA, boundary of empire, trade routes, AFRICA, Alexandria, CYRENAICA, AEGYPTUS, ivory, cinnamon, pepper

Travelers from Greece or Italy would approach Alexandria by sea. From 70 miles (88 kilometers) away, they would be welcomed by a beacon from the Pharos, a huge lighthouse named for the little island on which it stood. Like the Statue of Liberty on Liberty Island in New York Harbor, Pharos marked the entrance to a safe ocean port at the mouth of a great river, each beacon lighting the way to a vast cosmopolitan center. The three-tiered marble-faced Pharos was one of the seven wonders of the ancient world. Day and night the fire in the lantern level sent out a blaze of light which, enhanced by highly polished bronze mirrors, guided the thousands of ships that used the port each year.

Alexander's architect planned the city carefully, with its streets set out in a grid system, crossing each other at right angles as in many modern North American cities. The main street, Canopus Street, was more than 100 feet (30 meters) wide, wider than any street in Rome and four times the size of any street that Quintus would have known in Pompeii. Some of the houses were several stories high, and many of the public buildings were built of marble. By the Great Harbor was the Royal Quarter, an area of more than one square mile (260 hectares) containing palaces, temples, administrative offices, and gardens. West of the Royal Quarter was the Caesareum, where Quintus, in the paragraph on page 77, made his offering of wine. The Caesareum was a shrine begun by Queen Cleopatra in honor of the Roman general Mark Antony and completed by the Emperor Augustus as a temple dedicated to himself. In the words of the Jewish writer Philo, it was "wonderfully high and large, full of precious paintings and statues, and beautiful all over with gold and silver; it contains colonnades, libraries, courtyards, and sacred groves, all made as skillfully as possible with no expense spared."

Alexandria and trade in the first century AD.

The Pharos

Right: *Model of the Pharos based on evidence like the coin on page 86, with a cutaway drawing.*

The Pharos was over 440 feet (135 meters) high, with a fire constantly alight at the top. A spiral ramp inside the lowest stage allowed fuel to be carried up by animals. Statues of Ptolemy II and his queen can be seen at the base of the lighthouse.

Below: *A fifteenth-century fort was built on the ruins of the Pharos.*

In front of the Caesareum stood two obelisks, tall narrow pillars of granite, pointed at the top. They were brought from an ancient Egyptian temple and put in position by a Roman engineer in 13 BC. In the nineteenth century one was removed to London, England, and the other was taken to Central Park, New York City. They are known as Cleopatra's Needles.

But Alexandria was more than a city of fine streets, glittering marble, and busy trading; it was a center of education and study. The university, known as the Museum and situated in the Royal Quarter, had the largest library in the ancient world with more than half a million volumes on its shelves. As well as the Great Library, the Museum had lecture halls, laboratories, observatories, a park, and a zoo. Professional scholars were employed to do research in a wide range of subjects – mathematics, astronomy, anatomy, geography, literature, and languages. Here mapping techniques were improved, based on travelers' reports; here Euclid wrote his famous geometry textbook, and Aristarchus put forward his theory that the Earth goes round the Sun.

Alexandria was a city of many different races, including Egyptians, Jews, Romans, Africans, and Indians. But on the whole the people with most power and influence were the Greeks. They had planned the city and built it; they had ruled it before the Romans came and continued to play a part in running it under the Romans; theirs was the official language; they owned great wealth in Alexandria and enjoyed many privileges. This caused jealousy among the other races, and was one of the reasons why quarrels and riots frequently broke out. The Roman governor, or even the emperor himself, often had to step in and try to settle such disputes as fairly and peacefully as possible.

Cleopatra's Needle in London, England.

The Caesareum obelisks as they appeared at the end of the eighteenth century; in the bottom right-hand corner you can see that one is lying on the ground, partially buried.

After one violent riot, the Emperor Claudius included the following stern warning in a letter to the Alexandrians:

> *Although I am very angry with those who stirred up the trouble, I am not going to enquire fully into who was responsible for the riot – I might have said, the war – with the Jews. But I tell you this, once and for all: if you do not stop quarreling with each other, I shall be forced to show you what even a kind emperor can do when he has good reason to be angry.*

This mosaic floor comes from the dining room of a rich Alexandrian. It shows the head of Medusa, which could turn those who looked at it to stone.

Underwater Discoveries

Underwater excavations in the Great Harbor are now bringing much of the waterfront of ancient Alexandria back to life.

Top: *A diver examining a sphinx underwater.*

Above: *Raising part of a statue of one of the Greek rulers of Egypt, possibly Ptolemy II. The Pharos was completed in his reign.*

Right: *Several parts of the statue have been found, enabling it to be rebuilt. The huge figure, wearing the traditional royal dress of the Pharaohs, probably stood at the foot of the great lighthouse.*

Vocabulary checklist 17

Nouns in the checklists for Stages 17–20 are usually listed in the form of their nominative and genitive singular. Verbs are listed as before.

ā, ab	*from*	**īnsula, īnsulae**	*island*
animus, animī	*spirit, soul, mind*	**invītus**	*unwilling*
appropinquō, appropinquāre, appropinquāvī	*approach, come near to*	**itaque**	*and so*
		maximus	*very big*
		negōtium, negōtiī	*business*
āra, ārae	*altar*	**numquam**	*never*
bene	*well*	**paucī**	*few, a few*
benignus	*kind*	**perveniō, pervenīre, pervēnī**	*reach, arrive at*
diū	*for a long time*	**quondam**	*one day, once*
faber, fabrī	*craftsman*	**recipiō, recipere, recēpī**	*recover, take back*
facilis	*easy*		
graviter	*seriously*		
hūc	*here, to this place*	**resistō, resistere, restitī**	*resist*

Warships in a harbor. Wall painting from the temple of Isis at Pompeii.

EUTYCHUS
ET CLEMENS

Stage 18

Eutychus et Clēmēns

taberna

postquam ad urbem advēnimus, ego Clēmentī diū tabernam
quaerēbam. tandem Barbillus, quī multa aedificia possidēbat,
mihi tabernam optimam obtulit. haec taberna prope templum
deae Īsidis erat. in hāc parte urbis via est, in quā omnēs
tabernāriī vitrum vēndunt. taberna, quam Barbillus mihi
offerēbat, optimum situm habēbat. Barbillus tamen dubitābat.

"sunt multī latrōnēs," inquit, "in illā parte urbis. tabernāriī
latrōnēs timent, quod pecūniam extorquent et vim īnferunt.
latrōnēs lībertum meum interfēcērunt, quī nūper illam tabernam
tenēbat. eum in viā invēnimus mortuum. lībertus, quī senex
obstinātus erat, latrōnibus pecūniam dare nōluit. latrōnēs eum
necāvērunt tabernamque dīripuērunt."

"Clēmēns vir fortis, nōn senex īnfirmus est," ego Barbillō
respondī. "fortūna semper eī favet. hanc tabernam Clēmentī
emere volō. tibi centum aureōs offerō. placetne?"

"mihi placet," respondit Barbillus. "centum aureī sufficiunt."
Barbillō igitur centum aureōs trādidī.

5 **vitrum** *glass*
   situm: situs *position, site*
   dubitābat: dubitāre *be doubtful*
   latrōnēs: latrō *robber, thug*
   extorquent: extorquēre *extort*
10 **vim īnferunt: vim īnferre**
   use force, violence
   dīripuērunt: dīripere *ransack*
   īnfirmus *weak*
   fortūna *fortune, luck*
15 **centum aureōs** *a hundred gold*
   coins
   sufficiunt: sufficere *be enough*

latrōnēs eum necāvērunt.

in officīnā Eutychī

officīnā: officīna *workshop*

I

postquam tabernam Clēmentī dedī, ille mihi grātiās maximās
ēgit. statim ad viam, in quā taberna erat, festīnāvit: adeō
cupiēbat tabernam possidēre.

    in viā vitreāriōrum erat ingēns turba. ibi Clēmēns tabernam
suam prope templum Īsidis cōnspexit. valvās ēvulsās vīdit,   5
tabernam dīreptam. īrātus igitur Clēmēns tabernārium vīcīnum
rogāvit,

    "quis hoc fēcit?"

    tabernārius perterritus nōmina dare nōluit. tandem "rogā
Eutychum!" inquit.   10

    Clēmēns statim Eutychum quaesīvit. facile erat Clēmentī eum
invenīre, quod officīnam maximam possidēbat. prō officīnā
Eutychī stābant quattuor servī Aegyptiī. Clēmēns numquam
hominēs ingentiōrēs quam illōs Aegyptiōs vīderat. eōs tamen
nōn timēbat. ūnum servum ex ōrdine trāxit.   15

    "heus! Atlās!" inquit Clēmēns. "num dormīs? Eutychum,
dominum tuum, interrogāre volō. cūr mihi obstās? nōn decōrum
est tibi lībertō obstāre."

    tum Clēmēns servōs attonitōs praeteriit, et officīnam Eutychī
intrāvit.   20

adeō *so much, so greatly*

in viā vitreāriōrum
in the street of the glassmakers
valvās: valvae *doors*
ēvulsās: ēvulsus
     wrenched off
vīcīnum: vīcīnus
     neighboring, nearby
nōmina *names*
prō officīnā
     in front of the workshop
quattuor *four*

interrogāre *question*

praeteriit: praeterīre *go past*

II

Eutychus in lectō recumbēbat; cibum ē canistrō gustābat. valdē
sūdābat, et manūs in capillīs servī tergēbat. postquam
Clēmentem vīdit,

    "quis es, homuncule?" inquit. "quis tē hūc admīsit? quid vīs?"

    "Quīntus Caecilius Clēmēns sum," respondit Clēmēns. "dē   5
tabernā, quam latrōnēs dīripuērunt, cognōscere volō. nam illa
taberna nunc mea est."

    Eutychus, postquam hoc audīvit, Clēmentem amīcissimē
salūtāvit, et eum per officīnam dūxit. ipse Clēmentī fabrōs suōs
dēmōnstrāvit. in officīnā trīgintā vitreāriī Aegyptiī dīligenter   10
labōrābant; aderat vīlicus, quī virgam vibrābat.

    Eutychus, postquam Clēmentī officīnam ostendit, negōtium
agere coepit.

    "perīculōsum est, mī amīce, in viā vitreāriōrum," inquit. "multī
fūrēs ad hanc viam veniunt, multī latrōnēs. multa aedificia   15
dēlent. omnēs igitur tabernāriī auxilium ā mē petunt. tabernāriī mihi
pecūniam dant, ego eīs praesidium. tabernam tuam servāre
possum. omnēs tabernāriī mihi decem aureōs quotannīs dare solent.
paulum est. num tū praesidium meum recūsāre vīs?"

sūdābat: sūdāre *sweat*
manūs . . . tergēbat
     was wiping his hands
capillīs: capillī *hair*
admīsit: admittere *let in*

amīcissimē: amīcē
     in a friendly way

ā mē *from me*
praesidium *protection*

paulum *little*

Clēmēns tamen Eutychō nōn crēdēbat.

"ego ipse tabernam, in quā habitō, servāre possum," inquit Clēmēns. "praesidium tuum recūsō."

tum lībertus sēcūrus exiit.

sēcūrus *without a care*

Alexandria, home of luxury glass

Alexandrian glass was traded widely, even outside the Roman empire. The glass beaker on the right was made in Alexandria, but was found in Afghanistan. It has a painted design showing the princess Europa being carried off on the back of a bull, which is Jupiter in disguise.

The disc below is carved from glass in two layers, white on blue. We do not know where it was made, but the technique was probably used in Alexandria. It shows Paris pondering the judgment of Juno, Minerva, and Venus.

About the language 1: gender

1 You have already seen how an adjective changes its ending to agree, in case and number, with the noun it describes. For example:

ACCUSATIVE SINGULAR: rēx nūntium **fortem** salūtāvit.
The king greeted the brave messenger.

NOMINATIVE PLURAL: mercātōrēs **fessī** dormiēbant.
The tired merchants were sleeping.

2 An adjective agrees with the noun it describes not only in case and number but also in a third way, gender. All nouns in Latin belong to one of three genders: masculine, feminine, and neuter. Compare the following sentences:

Clēmēns amīcōs **callidōs** laudāvit.
Clemens praised the clever friends.

Clēmēns ancillās **callidās** laudāvit.
Clemens praised the clever slave girls.

In both sentences, the word for "clever" is accusative plural. But in the first sentence, the masculine form **callidōs** is used, because it describes **amīcōs**, which is masculine; in the second sentence, the feminine form **callidās** is used, because it describes **ancillās**, which is feminine.

3 The forms of the adjective which you have met are listed on page 158 in the Language information section.

Detail of a mosaic panel, including colored glass pieces.

4 Further examples:

a "ubi est coquus novus?" rogāvit Barbillus.
b "ubi est templum novum?" rogāvit Quīntus.
c magnae nāvēs ad portum Alexandrīae nāvigābant.
d tabernāriī ignāvī per fenestrās spectābant.
e nūntius dominō crūdēlī epistulam trādidit.
f mīlitēs latrōnem in vīllā mercātōris Graecī invēnērunt.

Write down the Latin noun and adjective pair in each sentence and use the Vocabulary in the Language information section to find the gender of each noun and adjective pair.

5 The Latin word for "who" or "which" at the beginning of a relative clause changes like an adjective to match the gender of the word it describes. Notice how the forms of **quī** (masculine), **quae** (feminine), and **quod** (neuter) are used in the following examples:

> rēx, **quī** in aulā habitābat, caerimōniam nūntiāvit.
> *The king, who lived in the palace, announced a ceremony.*

> puella, **quae** per forum contendēbat, latrōnēs vīdit.
> *The girl, who was hurrying through the forum, saw the thugs.*

> dōnum, **quod** āthlētam valdē dēlectāvit, erat statua.
> *The gift, which pleased the athlete very much, was a statue.*

6 Nouns such as **pater**, **fīlius**, **rēx**, which refer to males, are usually masculine; nouns such as **māter**, **fīlia**, **uxor**, which refer to females, are usually feminine. Other nouns can be masculine (e.g. **hortus**), feminine (e.g. **nāvis**), or neuter (e.g. **nōmen**).

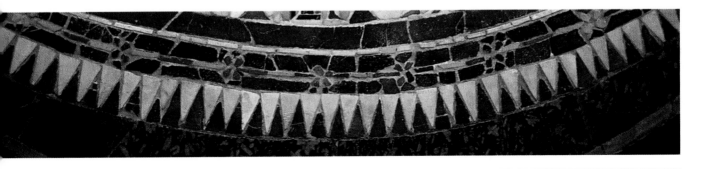

Clēmēns tabernārius

When you have read this story, answer the questions on page 101.

Clēmēns mox tabernam suam renovāvit. fabrōs condūxit, quī
valvās mūrōsque refēcērunt. multa ōrnāmenta vitrea ēmit.
cēterī tabernāriī, quamquam Eutychum valdē timēbant, Clēmentem
libenter adiuvābant. nam Clēmēns cōmis erat et eīs saepe
auxilium dabat. facile erat eī lucrum facere, quod pretia aequa   5
semper postulābat.

    haec taberna, ut dīxī, prope templum deae Īsidis erat. ad hoc
templum Clēmēns, quī pius erat, cotīdiē adībat. ibi deam Īsidem
adōrābat et eī ōrnāmentum vitreum saepe cōnsecrābat.

    sacerdōtēs, quī templum administrābant, mox Clēmentem   10
cognōvērunt. deinde Clēmēns Īsiacīs sē coniūnxit. sacerdōtēs eī
librum sacrum dedērunt, in quō dē mystēriīs deae legere
poterat. Clēmēns in templō cum sacerdōtibus cēnāre solēbat. in
cellā templī habitābat fēlēs sacra. Clēmēns eam semper
mulcēbat, et eī semper aliquid ex paterā suā dabat.   15

    mox plūrimōs amīcōs Clēmēns habēbat. nam tabernāriī, quī
Eutychō pecūniam invītī dabant, paulātim Clēmentī
cōnfīdēbant. tabernāriī Eutychum inimīcum putābant,
Clēmentem vindicem. tandem omnēs Eutychō pecūniam trādere
nōluērunt.   20

renovāvit: renovāre *restore*	
condūxit: condūcere *hire*	
refēcērunt: reficere *repair*	
ōrnāmenta: ōrnāmentum	
	ornament
vitrea: vitreus	
	glass, made of glass
lucrum *profit*	
aequa: aequus *fair*	
ut *as*	
pius *respectful to the gods*	
adōrābat: adōrāre *worship*	
cōnsecrābat: cōnsecrāre	
	dedicate
Īsiacīs: Īsiacus *follower of*	
	Isis
sē coniūnxit: sē coniungere	
	join
sacrum: sacer *sacred*	
mystēriīs: mystēria	
	mysteries, secret worship
mulcēbat: mulcēre *pet, pat*	
paterā: patera *bowl*	
cōnfīdēbant: cōnfīdere *trust*	
putābant: putāre	
	think, consider
vindicem: vindex	
	champion, defender

Eutychus, ubi dē hīs rēbus cognōvit, latrōnēs collēgit et eīs fūstēs dedit.

"iste Clēmēns," inquit Eutychus, "molestissimus est. necesse est eī poenās dare. ille impetūs nostrōs diūtius vītāvit."

latrōnēs, postquam fūstēs cēpērunt, ad tabernam Clēmentis contendērunt.

collēgit: colligere
    gather, collect
poenās dare *pay the penalty, be punished*
25 diūtius *for too long*

Questions

1 How did Clemens get his store repaired?
2 Why did the other storekeepers help Clemens (lines 3–5)?
3 Where was Clemens' store? Why was this convenient for Clemens (lines 7–8)?
4 How did he show his respect for the goddess (lines 8–9)?
5 How did the priests help Clemens to learn more about the goddess (lines 11–13)?
6 Where did the sacred cat live? In what ways did Clemens show kindness to it?
7 **mox plūrimōs amīcōs Clēmēns habēbat** (line 16). Who were these friends?
8 From line 18, pick out the Latin word that shows how Clemens' friends regarded Eutychus. How did they finally oppose Eutychus?
9 What conclusion did Eutychus come to about Clemens (lines 23–24)? Give two details.
10 Read the last sentence. Suggest two things the thugs might do.

prō tabernā Clēmentis

Clēmēns in templō deae Īsidis cum cēterīs Īsiacīs saepe cēnābat. quondam, ubi ā templō, in quō cēnāverat, domum redībat, amīcum cōnspexit accurrentem.

"taberna ardet! taberna tua ardet!" clāmāvit amīcus. "tabernam tuam dīripiunt Eutychus et latrōnēs. eōs vīdī valvās ēvellentēs, 5 vitrum frangentēs, tabernam incendentēs. fuge! fuge ex urbe! Eutychus tē interficere vult. nēmō eī latrōnibusque resistere potest."

Clēmēns tamen nōn fūgit, sed ad tabernam quam celerrimē contendit. postquam illūc advēnit, prō tabernā stābat immōtus. 10 valvās ēvulsās, tabernam dīreptam vīdit. Eutychus extrā tabernam cum latrōnibus Aegyptiīs stābat, rīdēbatque. Eutychus cachinnāns

"mī dulcissime!" inquit. "nōnne tē dē hāc viā monuī? nōnne amīcōs habēs quōs vocāre potes? cūr absunt? fortasse 15 sapientiōrēs sunt quam tū."

Clēmēns cum summā tranquillitāte eī respondit,

"absunt amīcī, sed deī mē servāre possunt. deī hominēs scelestōs pūnīre solent."

Eutychus īrātissimus 20 "quid dīcis?" inquit. "tūne mihi ita dīcere audēs?"

tum Eutychus latrōnibus signum dedit. statim quattuor Aegyptiī cum fūstibus Clēmentī appropinquābant. Clēmēns cōnstitit. via, in quā stābat, erat dēserta. tabernāriī perterritī per valvās tabernārum spectābant. omnēs invītī Clēmentem 25 dēseruerant, simulatque Eutychus et latrōnēs advēnērunt.

subitō fēlēs sacra, quam Clēmēns mulcēre solēbat, ē templō exiit. Clēmentem rēctā petīvit. in umerum Clēmentis īnsiluit. omnēs Aegyptiī statim fūstēs abiēcērunt et ad pedēs Clēmentis prōcubuērunt. Clēmentem, quem fēlēs sacra servābat, laedere 30 nōn audēbant.

saeviēbat Eutychus, sīcut taurus īrātus. tum fēlēs in Eutychum īnsiluit, et caput vehementer rāsit.

"melius est tibi fugere," inquit Clēmēns.

Eutychus cum latrōnibus perterritus fūgit. posteā neque 35 Clēmentem neque tabernāriōs laedere temptābat. nunc Clēmēns est prīnceps tabernāriōrum.

domum: domus *home*
accurrentem: accurrēns
     running up
ēvellentēs: ēvellēns
     wrenching off
frangentēs: frangēns *breaking*
incendentēs: incendēns
    burning, setting on fire
illūc *there, to that place*

monuī: monēre *warn*

sapientiōrēs: sapiēns *wise*
tranquillitāte: tranquillitās
     calmness
scelestōs: scelestus *wicked*

dēseruerant: dēserere *desert*
rēctā *directly, straight*
īnsiluit: īnsilīre *jump onto,*
     jump into
abiēcērunt: abicere *throw away*
laedere *harm*
sīcut taurus *like a bull*
rāsit: rādere *scratch*
neque . . . neque *neither . . . nor*
temptābat: temptāre *try*

Egyptian cats

The Egyptians kept cats both as pets and to control rats and mice in their granaries and food stores. They also venerated cats as sacred mammals as they thought they were earthly forms of the goddess Isis and another goddess called Bastet. When cats died they were mummified; vast numbers of them have been excavated.

Left: *This expensive bronze cat was made as an offering to the goddess Bastet around 600 BC.*

In Egyptian legend, each night a cat kills an evil snake that tries to prevent the sun from rising.

About the language 2: neuter nouns

1 Study the following examples:

   a plaustrum viam claudēbat.
   A cart was blocking the road.

   b plaustra viam claudēbant.
   Carts were blocking the road.

   c Vārica plaustrum ēmōvit.
   Varica removed the cart.

   d Vārica plaustra ēmōvit.
   Varica removed the carts.

2 **plaustrum** is a typical example of a **neuter noun**. The accusative singular of neuter nouns is always the same as the nominative singular (sentences a and c). The nominative and accusative plural of neuter nouns are also identical to each other, and they always end in **-a** (sentences b and d).

3 Compare the following forms:

	SECOND DECLENSION		THIRD DECLENSION	
	masculine	*neuter*	*masculine*	*neuter*
nominative singular	servus	templum	leō	nōmen
accusative singular	servum	templum	leōnem	nōmen
nominative plural	servī	templa	leōnēs	nōmina
accusative plural	servōs	templa	leōnēs	nōmina

4 Further examples:

   a Salvius horrea nova īnspexit.
   b Cogidubnus pompam ad lītus dūxit.
   c prīncipēs dōna ad aulam tulērunt.
   d nōmenne senis mortuī scīs?
   e Plancus monumenta urbis dēmōnstrāvit.
   f animālia hospitēs terruērunt.

Practicing the language

1 Complete each sentence with the correct form of the adjective and then translate. Remember that adjectives agree with nouns in case, number, and gender. If you are unsure of the gender of a noun, you can check it in the Vocabulary at the back of the book.

   a . . . . tabernāriī Eutychō pecūniam dedērunt. (multī, multae)
   b latrōnēs senem . . . . necāvērunt. (obstinātum, obstinātam)
   c Quīntus templum . . . . vīsitāvit. (magnificam, magnificum)
   d Aegyptiī Graecōs . . . . petīvērunt. (perterritōs, perterritās)
   e faber . . . . ad casam mē invītāvit. (benignus, benigna)
   f mercātor lībertō . . . . praemium obtulit. (fidēlī, fidēlibus)
   g Eutychus officīnam . . . . habēbat. (ingentem, ingēns)
   h servus ē vīllā dominī . . . . fūgit. (crūdēlem, crūdēlis)

2 Complete each sentence with the correct form of the noun or phrase and then translate.

   a . . . . , quam Clēmēns possidēbat, in viā vitreāriōrum erat. (taberna, tabernae)
   b . . . . , quī templum administrābant, Clēmentī librum sacrum dedērunt. (sacerdōtēs, sacerdōs)
   c in templō, quod prope tabernam Clēmentis erat, habitābat . . . . (fēlēs sacra, fēlēs sacrae)
   d ubi Eutychus et latrōnēs advēnērunt, ... valdē timēbant. (tabernārius Graecus, cēterī tabernāriī)
   e . . . . ad templum Īsidis festīnāvit et Clēmentī dē tabernā nārrāvit. (amīcus fidēlis, amīcī Graecī)
   f . . . . ē templō Īsidis celeriter discessērunt et ad tabernam cucurrērunt. (amīcus fidēlis, duo amīcī)

3 Complete each sentence with the correct form of the verb and then translate.

   a Clēmēns ad tabernam, quam Quīntus . . . . , festīnāvit. (ēmerat, ēmerant)
   b ingēns turba, quae viam . . . . , tabernam spectābat. (complēverat, complēverant)
   c Clēmēns ad Eutychum, quī latrōnēs . . . . , contendit. (mīserat, mīserant)
   d Eutychus Clēmentem, quem servī nōn . . . . , amīcissimē salūtāvit. (terruerat, terruerant)
   e Eutychus dē tabernāriīs, quī praesidium . . . . , Clēmentī nārrāvit. (petīverat, petīverant)
   f Clēmēns tamen praesidium, quod Eutychus eī . . . . , recūsāvit. (obtulerat, obtulerant)

Pick out the Latin word for "who" or "which" (**quī**, **quae**, etc.) at the beginning of each relative clause. Which noun does it refer to? Write down the gender of each pair.

Glassmaking

In the stories in this Stage, Quintus established Clemens in what is thought to have been one of Alexandria's oldest and most successful industries – glassmaking. The earliest Egyptian glass vessels, discovered in tombs, date from about 1500 BC, and glass continued to be made in Egypt through the period of the Pharaohs, the Ptolemaic kings, and the Roman conquest and occupation.

Glass is made from sand, plant ash or natron, and lime. The earliest use of glass was as a colored, opaque, or transparent glaze applied to ceramics before they were fired (as is still done today). Small pieces of colored glass were considered valuable and often rivaled precious gems as jewelry items.

As time passed, it was discovered – perhaps by a potter – that if glass is heated until it becomes semiliquid, it can be shaped and left to cool in a new, solid, independently standing shape. At first this shaping was carried out by wrapping a coil of molten glass around a clay or sand core. This core had been molded around a rod into the shape of a vase or any other object which was required. When the glass had cooled, the rod was pulled out from the core and the remaining parts of the core were scraped or washed out. This method was suitable only for making small luxury items, such as perfume containers.

A scent bottle made around a sand core.

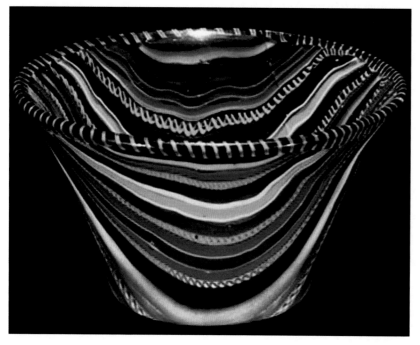

This ribbon-glass bowl was made by lining a mold with differently colored sticks of glass, then heating them until they melted and fused together.

This bowl is decorated in a typical Alexandrian style known as "millefiori" (Italian for "a thousand flowers"). Small pieces of colored glass were arranged in a mold and then heated until they fused together.

As the art of glassmaking progressed, glassmakers developed a second technique known as casting and cutting. In this process, glass was cast into a mold the approximate shape of the object desired. When the blank cooled, excess glass was cut away by a workman using a hand lathe or other tools. Magnificent specimens such as cameo glass and cage cups were created by ancient craftsmen using this technique. Variations on the casting technique were used in the creation of millefiori glass in which short sections of multicolored canes were placed into a mold and heated and fused, or ribbon glass, in which heated canes were sagged over a mold until they fused. As was the case with core forming, these techniques were labor-intensive and time-consuming, had a high breakage rate, and therefore resulted in expensive products.

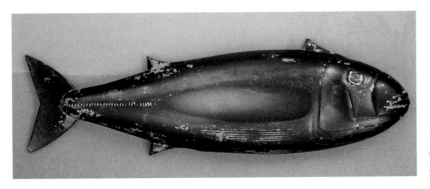

When this fish-shaped glass cover was removed, an actual cooked fish would be found underneath.

In the first century BC, somewhere at the eastern end of the Mediterranean, a new invention caused a true revolution in the glass industry. This was the discovery of glassblowing, both free blowing and mold blowing. The line drawing on the bottom left of this page demonstrates the process of free blowing. The craftsman at the back has picked up a gob of molten glass on the end of a hollow iron rod. The craftsman at the front has produced a hollow bubble of glass by blowing steadily through his rod. With repeated heating and blowing, the bubble can be made quite large and even shaped by swinging or by using various tools. Then the glassworker can add handles, bases, and decorations, such as trails of colored glass applied like piped icing on a cake. The very same processes are still in use today in modern facilities.

In the mold blowing technique, hot glass is blown into a mold, then shaped and finished as in free blowing. With the invention of free blowing and mold blowing, the earlier methods died out almost completely. Since glassblowing was faster and less labor-intensive, with low production costs, it was the basis of the mass production which characterized the Roman industry and made glass vessels more readily available and affordable.

A modern glassblower at work.

The color of "natural" glass is green to bluish-green. This color is caused by the varying amounts of naturally occurring iron impurities in the sand. Glassmakers learned to make colored glass by adding metallic compounds and mineral oxides to produce brilliant hues of red, green, and blue – the colors of gemstones. Glassmakers also learned to decolor glass to neutralize the effects of the impurities in the sand. When gemcutters learned to cut glass, they found that clear glass was an excellent refractor of light. The popularity of cut clear glass soared, that of colored glass diminished.

Soon after Alexandria's foundation it became a dominant center for the production of glass. With the introduction of glassblowing from the Near East, the industry spread within 150 years to Rome, northern Italy, Gaul, and the Rhineland with a widespread effect on most social classes. Glass tableware became common. The strength of glass, combined with its light weight, its resistance to retaining the odors and residue of its contents, and its transparency made glass containers reusable. Furthermore, about the time of our stories, the Romans discovered that panes could be made for windows out of glass instead of the more expensive quartz, thereby allowing architects to make windows larger and rooms brighter, especially in the **thermae** where illumination was dependent on oil lamps.

The art and skill of the ancient glassmakers were not equaled or surpassed in Europe until the rise of the Venetian glass industry during the Renaissance. In fact, the ancient methods of making cameo glass, gold band glass, and the cage cups were not duplicated until the late nineteenth and the twentieth centuries.

A blown jug in white glass with trailed decoration in blue.

This small scent bottle in the shape of a bunch of grapes is made of purple glass which has been blown into a mold.

A bubble of clear bluish glass has been shaped into a bird.

The Nile. Notice the fertile agricultural land between the desert and the river.

Egypt

South of Alexandria stretched the fertile valley of the river Nile. Every year the Nile flooded, watering the land and depositing rich new soil on the fields. This produced not only enough grain to supply the whole of Egypt but also a large surplus to be exported. However, the profits from the grain trade benefited only a small number of people.

Before the Romans came to Egypt, the country had been ruled by Egyptian "pharaohs" (kings), then by Persians, then by Greeks. These rulers had worked out a system for making the fullest possible use of the land for their own advantage. They regarded the whole country as their own property and treated the peasant farmers as their private force of workers. The peasants were not allowed to leave their villages without permission; they had to plant whatever crop they were told; and they did not receive their share of the harvest until the ruler had received his. They were also responsible for the upkeep and repair of the country's canals and dikes. In addition, the Egyptians were taxed to provide money needed to maintain the Pharos, the police, and the huge numbers of government officials who continually checked all activities of the people.

When the Romans came, they did nothing to improve the life of the peasants. Like the previous rulers, the Romans were more concerned with using the land for their own benefit than with improving the working conditions of peasant farmers. Above all, they wanted to ensure a steady supply of grain to Rome. Without the grain from Egypt and North Africa, the huge population of Rome would have starved and rioted. To avoid this danger the emperors made sure that Egypt was under their personal control.

Peasants harvesting wheat under supervision.

Everything the peasants did was checked by the officials.

Given these conditions and the fact that the Greek and Roman communities had special legal and tax privileges, it is not surprising that many letters of complaint have been found addressed by peasants to government officials; that bribery and corruption were common; and that, as in the story in Stage 17, there was social and racial unrest in Alexandria.

The Romans not only imported grain, papyrus, gold, marble, and granite from Egypt. They were also influenced by Egyptian culture. The worship of Serapis, Isis, and Osiris was enthusiastically adopted all over the Roman world. In imitation of the ancient pharaohs, Roman emperors had their names inscribed in hieroglyphs in the temples they built in Egypt where they might be portrayed in the Egyptian fashion, for instance, as the hawk-headed god, Horus. The Emperor Trajan built a Kiosk, complete with Egyptian architectural features, beside the sanctuary of Isis on the island of Philae near Egypt's southern border. Egypt was also a pleasure ground for upper-class Romans and we can imagine Quintus sailing up the Nile some 100 miles (160 kilometers) from Alexandria to the Giza plateau, lured by the ancient wonders of the Sphinx and the pyramids built thousands of years before his time.

Emperor as Horus. This hawk-headed emperor wears Roman sandals and a toga.

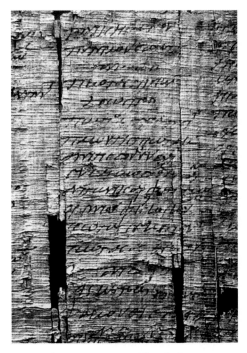

Part of an Egyptian official document. This papyrus was written in Greek during the Roman period of rule, and concerns work done on a canal.

The god of the Nile bearing the river's rich harvest.

Vocabulary checklist 18

The gender of each noun will now be indicated.

audeō, audēre	*dare*	**mīles, mīlitis, m.**	*soldier*
caput, capitis, n.	*head*	**nam**	*for*
coepī	*I began*	**nēmō**	*no one*
cognōscō, cognōscere, cognōvī	*get to know, find out*	**obstō, obstāre, obstitī**	*obstruct, block the way*
dea, deae, f.	*goddess*	**pars, partis, f.**	*part*
dēmōnstrō, dēmōnstrāre, dēmōnstrāvī	*point out, show*	**petō, petere, petīvī**	*beg for, ask for*
discēdō, discēdere, discessī	*depart, leave*	**posteā**	*afterwards*
fortasse	*perhaps*	**prō**	*in front of*
ibi	*there*	**quō?**	*where? where to?*
libenter	*gladly*	**recūsō, recūsāre, recūsāvī**	*refuse*
manus, manūs, f.	*hand*	**soleō, solēre**	*be accustomed*

A Roman mosaic uses millefiori glass pieces for the clothes of these Egyptian characters.

ISIS

Stage 19

1 hic vir est Aristō. Aristō est amīcus
   Barbillī. in vīllā splendidā habitat, sed
   miserrimus est.

2 haec fēmina est Galatēa. Galatēa est uxor
   Aristōnis. Galatēa marītum saepe
   vituperat, numquam laudat.

3 haec puella est Helena. Helena est fīlia
   Aristōnis et Galatēae. multī iuvenēs hanc
   puellam amant, quod pulcherrima est.

4 pompa splendida per viās Alexandrīae
prōcēdit. omnēs Alexandrīnī hanc
pompam spectāre volunt.

5 hī virī sunt sacerdōtēs deae Īsidis. Aristō
hōs virōs intentē spectat. sacerdōtēs
statuam deae per viās portant.

6 hae puellae prō pompa currunt. Helena
hās puellās intentē spectat. puellae
corōnās rosārum gerunt.

7 pompa ad templum Serāpidis advenit.
prope hoc templum stant duo iuvenēs. hī
iuvenēs tamen pompam nōn spectant.

Aristō

Aristō vir miserrimus est, quod vītam dūram vīvit. pater
Aristōnis scrīptor nōtissimus erat, quī in Graeciā habitābat.
tragoediās optimās scrībēbat. Aristō, quod ipse tragoediās
scrībere vult, vītam quiētam quaerit; sed uxor et fīlia eī obstant.

Galatēa, uxor Aristōnis, amīcōs ad vīllam semper invītat.   5
amīcī Galatēae sunt tībīcinēs et citharoedī. hī amīcī in vīllā
Aristōnis semper cantant et iocōs faciunt. Aristō amīcōs uxōris
semper fugit.

Helena quoque, fīlia Aristōnis et Galatēae, patrem vexat.
multōs iuvenēs ad vīllam patris invītat. amīcī Helenae sunt   10
poētae. in vīllā Aristōnis poētae versūs suōs recitant. Aristō hōs
versūs nōn amat, quod scurrīlēs sunt. saepe poētae inter sē
pugnant. saepe Aristō amīcōs fīliae ē vīllā expellit. difficile est
Aristōnī tragoediās scrībere.

dūram: dūrus *hard, harsh*
vīvit: vīvere *live*
scrīptor *writer*
tragoediās: tragoedia *tragedy*

tībīcinēs: tībīcen *pipe player*
citharoedī: citharoedus
cithara player

expellit: expellere *throw out*

The Roman theater at Alexandria.

A writer of plays.

diēs fēstus

diēs fēstus *festival, holiday*

I

cīvēs laetī erant. nam hiems erat cōnfecta. iam prīmus diēs vēris erat. iam sacerdōtēs deam Īsidem per viās urbis ad portum ferre solēbant. pompa, quam plūrimī Alexandrīnī spectāre volēbant, splendida erat.

hanc pompam tamen Barbillus spectāre nōlēbat.   5

"nōn commodum est mihi hodiē ad urbem īre," inquit. "ego hanc pompam saepe vīdī, tū tamen numquam. amīcus meus igitur, Aristō, tē ad pompam dūcere vult."

Barbillō grātiās ēgī, et cum Aristōne ad portum ībam. Galatēa et fīlia, Helena, nōbīscum ībant. viās urbis iam complēbant cīvēs   10
Alexandrīnī. ubi portuī appropinquābāmus, Galatēa fīliam et marītum assiduē vituperābat:

"Helena! nōlī festīnāre! tolle caput! Aristō! ēmovē hanc turbam! turba Alexandrīnōrum tōtam viam complet. in magnō perīculō sumus."   15

cōnfecta: **cōnfectus** *finished*
vēris: **vēr** *spring*
Alexandrīnī: Alexandrīnus *Alexandrian*

assiduē *continually*
tolle! *hold up!*

This portrait of a young woman called Eirene ("Peace") might help us to picture Helena in our stories. Portraits like this (and those on pages 118–119) used to be attached to Egyptian mummies during the Roman period. They enable us to visualize the varied faces in the Alexandrian crowd at the festival of Isis.

II

When you have read this part of the story, answer the questions on page 119.

postquam ad templum Augustī vēnimus, Galatēa
    "locum optimum nōvimus," inquit, "unde tōtum spectāculum   **unde** *from where*
vidēre solēmus. servus nōbīs illum locum servat. Aristō! nōnne
servum māne ēmīsistī?"
    "ēheu!" Aristō sibi dīxit.   5
    ubi ad illum locum, quem Galatēa ēlēgerat, tandem
pervēnimus, Galatēa duōs iuvenēs cōnspexit. hī iuvenēs locum
tenēbant, ubi Galatēa stāre volēbat.
    "marīte!" exclāmāvit. "ēmovē illōs iuvenēs! ubi est servus
noster? nōnne servum ēmīsistī?"   10
    "cārissima," respondit Aristō, quī anxius circumspectābat,
"melius est nōbīs locum novum quaerere. iste servus sānē   **sānē** *obviously*
neglegēns erat."
    Galatēa tamen, quae iam īrātissima erat, Aristōnem incitāvit.
ille igitur iuvenibus appropinquāvit et cōmiter locum poscēbat.   15 **cōmiter** *politely, courteously*
uxor tamen vehementer clāmāvit,
    "iuvenēs! cēdite! nōlīte nōbīs obstāre!"
    iuvenēs, quamquam rem graviter ferēbant, cessērunt. iuvenēs   **avidī: avidus** *eager*
Galatēam spectābant timidī, Helenam avidī.
    subitō spectātōrēs pompam cōnspexērunt. statim multitūdō   20
spectātōrum clāmōrem sustulit.
    "ecce pompa! ecce! dea Īsis!"

Questions

1 **ad templum Augustī vēnimus**. Write down one thing you already know about this temple.

2 **locum optimum nōvimus** (line 2). Why did Galatea describe the place as **optimum**?

3 What was the slave's job?

4 Why do you think Aristo said "**ēheu!**" to himself?

5 In lines 6–8, what unpleasant surprise did Galatea have?

6 What did Galatea tell her husband to do? What suspicion did she have (lines 9–10)?

7 What alternative suggestion did Aristo make? How did he try to avoid blame?

8 After going up to the young men, how did Aristo carry out his wife's instruction?

9 What did Galatea do that showed her attitude was different from her husband's? What did she tell the young men to do (line 17)?

10 Why do you think they finally gave up the place (lines 18–19)?

11 Why do you think Galatea at last stopped nagging everyone?

12 Having read this part of the story, how would you describe Aristo's character? Make three points and give evidence for each one.

About the language 1: *hic* and *ille*

1 You have now met the following forms of the Latin word for "this"
(plural "these"):

	SINGULAR			PLURAL	
	masculine	*feminine*	*neuter*	*masculine*	*feminine*
nominative	hic	haec	hoc	hī	hae
accusative	hunc	hanc	hoc	hōs	hās

hic vir est Barbillus.	*This man is Barbillus.*
hanc pompam vīdī.	*I saw this procession.*
hae stolae sunt sordidae!	*These dresses are dirty!*
tibi **hōs** flōrēs trādō.	*I hand these flowers to you.*

2 You have also met the following forms of the Latin word for "that"
(plural "those"):

	SINGULAR			PLURAL	
	masculine	*feminine*	*neuter*	*masculine*	*feminine*
nominative	ille	illa	illud	illī	illae
accusative	illum	illam	illud	illōs	illās

illa fēmina est Galatēa.	*That woman is Galatea.*
Clēmēns **illōs** sacerdōtēs saepe adiuvābat.	*Clemens often used to help those priests.*
illae viae sunt perīculōsae.	*Those roads are dangerous.*
multī Aegyptiī **illud** templum vīsitābant.	*Many Egyptians used to visit that temple.*

3 Note that **hic** and **ille** agree in case, number, and gender with the
nouns they describe.

4 Further examples:

    a haec cēna est optima.
    b latrōnēs illum mercātōrem vituperant.
    c hoc templum prope forum est.
    d hī servī sunt Aegyptiī.
    e illud monumentum nōtissimum est.
    f ille iuvenis puellās vexat.

For a complete chart of the forms for **hic** and **ille**, see page 165.

pompa

*pompa adveniēbat. prō pompā currēbant multae puellae, quae flōrēs in
viam spargēbant. post multitūdinem puellārum tubicinēs et puerī
prōcēdēbant. puerī suāviter cantābant. tubicinēs tubās īnflābant. nōs,
quī pompam plānē vidēre poterāmus, assiduē plaudēbāmus. duo
iuvenēs tamen, quōs Galatēa ē locō ēmōverat, pompam vidēre vix
poterant.*

spargēbant: **spargere** *scatter*
tubicinēs: tubicen *trumpeter*
īnflābant: īnflāre *blow*
plānē *clearly*

5

Helena:	spectā illās rosās, quās fēminae in viam spargunt! rosās pulchriōrēs quam illās numquam vīdī.
iuvenis prīmus:	pompam vidēre nōn possum. sed spectā illam puellam! puellam pulchriōrem quam illam rārō vīdī.
Galatēa:	Helena! hūc venī! stā prope mē! Aristō! cūr fīliam tuam in tantā multitūdine nōn cūrās?

rosās: **rosa** *rose*

10

rārō *rarely*

	(subitō omnēs tubicinēs tubās vehementer īnflābant.)	*15*
Galatēa:	ō mē miseram! ō caput meum! audīte illōs tubicinēs! audīte illum sonitum! quam raucus est sonitus tubārum!	**sonitum: sonitus** *sound* **raucus** *harsh*
iuvenis secundus:	tubicinēs vix audīre possum. quam raucae sunt vōcēs fēminārum Graecārum! *20*	**vōcēs: vōx** *voice*
	(post turbam puerōrum tubicinumque vēnit dea ipsa. quattuor sacerdōtēs effigiem deae in umerīs ferēbant.)	
Galatēa:	spectā illam stolam! pulcherrima est illa *25* stola, pretiōsissima quoque. ēheu! vīlēs sunt omnēs stolae meae, quod marītus avārus est.	**vīlēs: vīlis** *cheap*
	(subitō iuvenēs, quī effigiem vidēre nōn poterant, Galatēam trūsērunt. iuvenis forte 30 pedem Galatēae calcāvit.)	**trūsērunt: trūdere** *push, shove* **calcāvit: calcāre** *step on*
	ō iuvenem pessimum nōlī mē vexāre! nōn decōrum est mātrōnam trūdere. num bēstia es?	**mātrōnam: mātrōna** *lady*
Helena:	māter! hic iuvenis forte tibi nocuit. *35* spectātōrēs nōs premunt, quod pompam vidēre cupiunt.	**nocuit: nocēre** *hurt* **premunt: premere** *push*
Galatēa:	Helena! nōlī istum iuvenem dēfendere! īnsolentissimus est. Aristō! cūr mē nōn servās? uxōrem filiamque numquam cūrās. *40* miserrima sum!	
Aristō:	ēheu! uxor mē vexat, filia mātrem. clāmōrēs eārum numquam effugere possum. facile est mihi tragoediās scrībere. tōta vīta mea est tragoedia! *45*	**eārum** *their*

tōta vīta mea est tragoedia!

About the language 2: imperatives

1 In the following sentences, one or more persons are being told to do something:

> māter! **spectā** pompam!
> *Mother! Look at the procession!*

> māter! pater! **spectāte** pompam!
> *Mother! Father! Look at the procession!*

> Helena! **venī** ad mē!
> *Helena! Come to me!*

> servī! **venīte** ad mē!
> *Slaves! Come to me!*

The form of the verb in **boldface** is known as the imperative. If only one person is being told to do something, the imperative singular is used; if more than one person, the imperative plural is used.

2 Compare the imperative forms with the infinitive:

	IMPERATIVE		INFINITIVE
	SINGULAR	PLURAL	
first conjugation	portā!	portāte!	portāre
	carry!	*carry!*	*to carry*
second conjugation	docē!	docēte!	docēre
	teach!	*teach!*	*to teach*
third conjugation	trahe!	trahite!	trahere
	drag!	*drag!*	*to drag*
fourth conjugation	audī!	audīte!	audīre
	listen!	*listen!*	*to listen*

3 Study the way in which people are ordered **not** to do things:

SINGULAR	nōlī currere!	*don't run!*
	nōlī cantāre!	*don't sing!*
PLURAL	nōlīte festīnāre!	*don't hurry!*
	nōlīte trūdere!	*don't push!*

nōlī and **nōlīte** are the imperative forms of the verb **nōlō**. Notice that they are used with the infinitive. **nōlī currere** literally means "be unwilling to run" and so "don't run."

4 Further examples:

a iuvenēs! tacēte!
b dīligenter labōrā!
c date mihi pecūniam!
d mē adiuvā!
e nōlī dormīre!
f nōlīte discēdere!
g nōlīte Rōmānōs interficere!
h nōlī mē pūnīre!

In each example, state whether the order is given to one person or more than one.

hodiē sōl Arietī appropinquat. *According to legend, the heavens were supported on the shoulders of a giant, Atlas. In this sculpture of Atlas carrying the globe of the heavens, the constellation Aries (the Ram) can be seen towards the left, across three narrow parallel lines that mark the path of the Sun across the heavens.*

vēnātiō

I

Barbillus mē et Aristōnem ad vēnātiōnem invītāvit. māne vīlicum Phormiōnem cum multīs servīs ēmīsit. Phormiō sēcum duōs haedōs dūxit. sed, ubi ē vīllā discēdēbāmus, astrologus Barbillī commōtus ad nōs cucurrit.

"domine, quō festīnās?" clāmāvit. "cūr ē vīllā hodiē exīre vīs?"   5

"ad praedium meum iter facimus," Barbillus astrologō respondit.

"sed, domine," inquit astrologus, "immemor es. perīculōsum est tibi hodiē ē vīllā exīre, quod hodiē sōl Arietī appropinquat."

ubi hoc audīvī, astrologum dērīsī. Barbillus, quamquam eī   10
crēdēbat, mē offendere nōluit. postquam rem diū cōgitāvit,

"mihi placet exīre," inquit.

astrologus igitur, ubi dominō persuādēre nōn potuit, amulētum eī dedit. tum sēcūrī ad praedium Barbillī contendimus. per partem praediī flūmen Nīlus lēniter fluēbat.   15

ubi illūc advēnimus, multōs servōs vīdimus collēctōs. in hāc multitūdine servōrum erant nōnnūllī Aethiopes, quī hastās in manibus tenēbant. prope Aethiopas stābat Phormiō, vīlicus Barbillī.

Phormiō "salvē, domine!" inquit. "omnia tibi parāvimus.   20
scaphās, quās postulāvistī, comparāvimus."

"haedōs cecīdistis?" rogāvit Barbillus.

"duōs haedōs cecīdimus, domine," respondit vīlicus. "eōs in scaphās iam posuimus."

haedōs: haedus *kid, young goat*
astrologus *astrologer*
commōtus *alarmed, excited*
praedium *estate*
immemor *forgetful*
Arietī: Ariēs *the Ram (sign of the zodiac)*
offendere *displease*
persuādēre *persuade*
amulētum *amulet, lucky charm*
flūmen Nīlus *river Nile*
lēniter *gently*
collēctōs: collēctus *assembled*
Aethiopes *Ethiopians*
omnia *everything, all things*
scaphās: scapha *punt, small boat*
cecīdistis: caedere *kill*

II

tum Phormiō nōs ad rīpam flūminis dūxit, ubi scaphae, quās comparāverat, dēligātae erant. postquam scaphās cōnscendimus, ad palūdem, in quā crocodīlī latēbant, cautē nāvigāvimus. ubi mediae palūdī appropinquābāmus, Barbillus Phormiōnī signum dedit. haedōs Phormiō in aquam iniēcit. crocodīlī, ubi haedōs cōnspexērunt, praecipitēs eōs petēbant. tum Aethiopes crocodīlōs agitāre coepērunt. hastās ēmittēbant et crocodīlōs interficiēbant. magna erat fortitūdō crocodīlōrum, maior tamen perītia Aethiopum. mox multī crocodīlī mortuī erant.

   subitō ingentem clāmōrem audīvimus.

   "domine!" clāmāvit Phormiō. "hippopotamus, quem Aethiopes ē palūde excitāvērunt, scapham Barbillī ēvertit. Barbillum et trēs servōs in aquam dēiēcit."

   quamquam ad Barbillum et ad servōs, quī in aquā natābant, celeriter nāvigāvimus, crocodīlī iam eōs circumvēnerant. hastās in crocodīlōs statim ēmīsimus. ubi crocodīlōs dēpulimus, Barbillum et ūnum servum servāre potuimus. sed postquam Barbillum ex aquā trāximus, eum invēnimus vulnerātum. hasta, quam servus ēmīserat, umerum Barbillī percusserat. Barbillus ā servō suō graviter vulnerātus erat.

rīpam: rīpa *bank*
dēligātae: dēligātus *tied up, moored*
palūdem: palūs *marsh, swamp*
5 **crocodīlī: crocodīlus** *crocodile*
iniēcit: inicere *throw in*
praecipitēs: praeceps *headlong, straight for*
fortitūdō *courage*
10 **perītia** *skill*

hippopotamus *hippopotamus*
ēvertit: ēvertere *overturn*

15

dēpulimus: dēpellere *drive off*

20 **ā servō suō** *by his own slave*

A mosaic showing pygmies hunting a crocodile and hippos in the river Nile.

An amulet, in the form of the hippopotamus god Thueris.

About the language 3: vocative case

1 In each of the following sentences, somebody is being spoken to:

Aristō! quam stultus es!	*Aristo! How stupid you are!*
quid accidit, **Barbille**?	*What happened, Barbillus?*
contendite, **amīcī**!	*Hurry, friends!*
cūr rīdētis, **cīvēs**?	*Why are you laughing, citizens?*

The words in **boldface** are in the vocative case. If only one person is spoken to, the vocative singular is used; if more than one person, the vocative plural is used.

2 The vocative case has the same form as the nominative with the exception of the vocative singular of words in the second declension.

3 Compare the nominative singular and vocative singular of second declension nouns like **servus** and **Salvius**:

nominative	*vocative*
servus labōrat.	cūr labōrās, **serve**?
amīcus gladium habet.	dā mihi gladium, **amīce**!
Eutychus est in viā.	ubi sunt latrōnēs, **Eutyche**?
Salvius est īrātus.	quid accidit, **Salvī**?
fīlius currit.	cūr curris, **fīlī**?
Holcōnius in lectō recumbit.	**Holcōnī**! surge!

4 The vocative plural has the same form as the nominative plural:

nominative	*vocative*
custōdēs dormiunt.	vōs semper dormītis, **custōdēs**.
puerī in forō stant.	ubi est theātrum, **puerī**?
puellae ad pompam festīnant.	nōlīte currere, **puellae**!

A Nile crocodile in a painting in the temple of Isis at Pompeii.

1 Complete each sentence with the correct form of **hic** or **ille** and then translate. If you are not sure of the gender of a noun, you will find it in the Vocabulary at the end of the book.

   a .... astrologus Barbillō dē perīculō
     persuādēre nōn potuit. (hic, hoc)
   b Phormiō .... servōs ad flūmen Nīlum
     mīsit. (illōs, illās)
   c .... flūmen est perīculōsum. (hic, hoc)
   d .... servī prope flūmen stābant. (hī, hae)
   e Phormiō .... scaphās in rīpā īnstrūxit. (illōs, illās)
   f .... crocodīlī haedōs petīvērunt. (illī, illae)
   g Aethiopes .... hippopotamum
     ē palūde excitāvērunt. (illum, illam, illud)
   h .... hasta umerum Barbillī
     percussit. (hic, haec, hoc)

2 Using the table of nouns on pages 154–155 of the Language information section, complete these sentences by filling in the endings, and then translate. For example:

   mercātor in viā stābat. amīcī mercātōr. . . salūtāvērunt.
   mercātor in viā stābat. amīcī **mercātōrem** salūtāvērunt.
   A merchant was standing in the street. The friends greeted the merchant.

   a puella stolam habēbat. stola puell. . . erat splendidissima.
   b servus leōn. . . in silvā vīdit. leō dormiēbat.
   c puellae tabernam intrāvērunt. mercātor puell. . . multās stolās
     ostendit.
   d cīvēs rēgem laudāvērunt, quod rēx cīv. . . magnum
     spectāculum dederat.
   e serv. . . , quod dominum timēbant, fūgērunt.
   f multī cīvēs in casīs habitābant. casae cīv. . . erant sordidae.
   g servī dīligenter labōrāvērunt. serv. . . igitur praemium dedī.
   h puer perterritus ad templum cucurrit et iānuam templ. . .
     pulsāvit.
   i rē. . . , quī in aulā sedēbat, tubam audīvit.
   j Salvius puer. . . , quī amphorās portābant, vehementer
     vituperāvit.

The worship of Isis

Isis was one of Egypt's oldest and most important goddesses. The Egyptians worshipped Isis for her power to give new life. They believed that she was responsible for the new life which followed the annual flooding of the Nile waters, and that she offered a hope of life after death for those who became her followers.

One of the most important festivals of Isis was held at the beginning of spring. It took place annually on March 5th, when the sailing season opened and the large grain ships, so crucial to Rome's food supply, could once again set off safely across the Mediterranean. A statue of Isis was carried in procession down to the Great Harbor.

The procession was headed by dancers and musicians playing pipes, trumpets, and castanets. Female attendants scattered roses in the road and over the tightly-packed crowd. The statue of Isis was carried high on the shoulders of her priests, so that everyone could get a glimpse of the goddess and her splendid robe. Next came more priests and priestesses and more trumpeters, and finally the high priest, wearing garlands of roses and shaking a sacred rattle known as a **sistrum**.

At the harbor, a special newly-built ship was moored. Its stern was shaped like a goose's neck and covered with gold plate. First the high priest dedicated the ship to Isis and offered prayers; then the priests, priestesses, and people loaded it with gifts of spices and flowers; finally the mooring ropes were unfastened and the wind carried the ship out to sea.

After the ceremony at the harbor, the statue of Isis was taken back to the temple. The spectators crowded into the open area in front of the temple, and the priests replaced the statue in the **cella** or sanctuary. Then a priest read to the people from a sacred book and recited prayers for the safety of the Roman people and their emperor, and for sailors and ships.

Isis

According to the Egyptians, Isis loved her brother, the god Osiris who appeared on earth in the form of a man. However, Osiris was murdered. His body was cut up and the pieces were scattered throughout the world. Overcome with grief, Isis set out on a search for the pieces of Osiris' corpse. When at last she had found them all, a miracle took place: the dead Osiris was given new life and became the father of the child Horus. This is why the Egyptians worshipped Isis as a bringer of new life.

Isis was often portrayed as a loving mother, nursing her child, Horus.

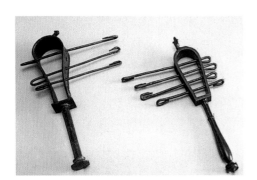

Two bronze sistra.

Woman holding a sistrum.

Above: *Isis, as the protector of shipping, holds a square sail in this Alexandrian coin. The Pharos can be seen on the right.*

Left: *Isis and her brother Osiris.*

Left: *Mosaic showing the Nile in flood. The Egyptians believed that Isis sent these floods, which brought Egypt its fertile soil.*

The festival was noisy and colorful. Everybody had the day off, and although the religious ceremony was serious, it was also good entertainment. When the ceremony was over, the Alexandrians continued to enjoy themselves. Their behavior was sometimes criticized, for example by the writer Philo:

> *They give themselves up to heavy drinking, noisy music, amusements, feasting, luxury, and rowdy behavior, eager for what is shameful and neglecting what is decent. They wake by night and sleep by day, turning the laws of nature upside down.*

But in spite of Philo's words, a festival of Isis was not just an excuse for a holiday. The worship of the goddess was taken seriously by many Egyptians, who went regularly to her temple, prayed to her statue, and made offerings. Some of them, like Clemens in Stage 18, went further and became **Īsiacī**, members of the special brotherhood of Isis. This involved a long period of preparation leading up to an initiation ceremony in the temple.

Those who wished to join the brotherhood of Isis had to begin with an act of repentance for the sins they had committed in the past; for example, they might offer a sacrifice, or abstain from food, or go on a pilgrimage. In a Latin novel known as *The Golden Ass*, the main character becomes a follower of Isis. He explains to his readers how he prepared to be admitted to the brotherhood. First his body was washed by the priests in a ceremony of baptism; next he was taught about the sacred mysteries of the goddess, and forbidden to reveal them to anyone outside the brotherhood; then he fasted for ten days before finally undergoing the initiation ceremony in the temple.

A ceremony outside a temple of Isis.

As the worship of Isis spread from Egypt into the Greek and Roman world, new ways were found of depicting the goddess, left. This Egyptian drawing shows her with her hieroglyph, a throne, above her head. She carries a scepter in one hand and an ankh, the symbol for life, in the other. On the right is a Roman painting of Isis holding the sacred cobra of Egypt. It was found in her temple at Pompeii.

This was a ceremony of mystery and magic, full of strange and emotional experiences for the worshippers. Those who were initiated believed that they had personally met Isis and that by dedicating themselves to her they could hope for life after death. But the exact details of the ceremony were kept strictly secret, as the narrator of *The Golden Ass* explains: "If you are interested in my story, you may want to know what was said and done in the temple. I would tell you if I were allowed to tell, you would learn if you were allowed to hear; but your ears and my tongue would suffer for your foolish curiosity."

By the time of our stories, the worship of Isis had spread from Alexandria across the ancient world. Temples to Isis have been found in places as far apart as London and around the Black Sea. A group of priests serving in a temple of Isis at Pompeii suffered a miserable death when the city was destroyed in the eruption of Vesuvius. They collected the sacred objects and treasures, and fled from the temple, but by then it was too late. Their bodies were found along the route of their flight across the city, each corpse surrounded by the valuables he had tried to save.

This food – nuts, grain, and bread – was found in the temple of Isis at Pompeii.

Vocabulary checklist 19

Adjectives from now on are usually listed as in the Language information section (see page 158).

amō, amāre, amāvī	*love, like*	**locus, locī, m.**	*place*
cārus, cāra, cārum	*dear*	**māne**	*in the morning*
cōgitō, cōgitāre, cōgitāvī	*think, consider*	**nōvī**	*I know*
comparō, comparāre, comparāvī	*obtain*	**perīculum, perīculī, n.**	*danger*
cōnficiō, cōnficere, cōnfēcī	*finish*	**plūrimī**	*very many*
cūrō, cūrāre, cūrāvī	*look after*	**poscō, poscere, poposcī**	*demand, ask for*
fluō, fluere, flūxī	*flow*	**tot**	*so many*
forte	*by chance*	**vexō, vexāre, vexāvī**	*annoy*
grātiās agō	*I thank, give thanks*	**vīvō, vīvere, vīxī**	*live*
hasta, hastae, f.	*spear*	**vix**	*hardly, scarcely*
illūc	*there, to that place*	**vōx, vōcis, f.**	*voice*
iter, itineris, n.	*journey*		

In Egyptian mythology, the male hippo was identified with Seth, the god of storms and the enemy of Isis and Osiris. Small figures like this are often found in tombs.

MEDICUS

Stage 20

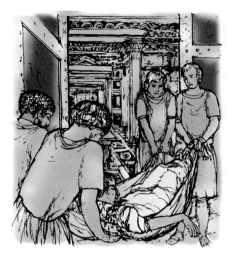

1 servī ad vīllam revēnērunt, Barbillum portantēs.

ancillae prope lectum stābant, lacrimantēs.

3 astrologus in cubiculum irrūpit, clāmāns.

4 Barbillus, in lectō recumbēns, astrologum audīvit.

5 Phormiō ad urbem contendit, medicum quaerēns.

remedium astrologī

ego et servī cum Barbillō ad vīllam quam celerrimē rediimus.
multus sanguis ex vulnere Barbillī effluēbat. Phormiō, quī servōs
vulnerātōs sānāre solēbat, tunicam suam sciderat; partem
tunicae circum umerum Barbillī dēligāverat. fluēbat tamen
sanguis. 5

servī, quī Barbillum portābant, ubi cubiculum intrāvērunt, in
lectum eum lēniter posuērunt. duae ancillae prope lectum
stābant lacrimantēs. Phormiō ancillās ē cubiculō ēmīsit et servōs
ad sē vocāvit.

"necesse est vōbīs," inquit, "magnum numerum arāneārum 10
quaerere. ubi sanguis effluit, nihil melius est quam arāneae."

servī per tōtam vīllam contendēbant, arāneās quaerentēs;
magnum clāmōrem tollēbant. Phormiō, postquam servī multās
arāneās ad cubiculum tulērunt, in umerum dominī eās
collocāvit. 15

astrologus ancillās lacrimantēs vīdit, servōsque clāmantēs
audīvit. statim in cubiculum Barbillī irrūpit, exclāmāns:

"nōnne hoc prōvīdī? ō nefāstum diem! ō dominum īnfēlīcem!"

"habēsne remedium?" rogāvī anxius.

"remedium certum habeō," respondit astrologus. "facile est 20
mihi Barbillum sānāre, quod nōs astrologī sumus vērī medicī.
prīmō necesse est mihi mūrem nigrum capere. deinde mūrem
captum dissecāre volō. postrēmō eum in umerum Barbillī
pōnere volō. hoc sōlum remedium est."

subitō, Barbillus, quī astrologum audīverat, oculōs aperuit. 25
postquam mihi signum languidum dedit, in aurem meam
susurrāvit,

"quaere Petrōnem, medicum bonum!"

Phormiōnem, quī Petrōnem bene nōverat, ē vīllā statim ēmīsī.
itaque vīlicus medicum quaerēbat, astrologus mūrem. 30

remedium *cure*

vulnere: vulnus *wound*
effluēbat: effluere *pour out, flow out*
sānāre *heal, cure*
sciderat: scindere *tear up*
dēligāverat: dēligāre *bind, tie*
lectum: lectus *bed*

numerum: numerus *number*
arāneārum: arānea *spider's web*

tollēbant: tollere *raise*

collocāvit: collocāre *place*

prōvīdī: prōvidēre *foresee*
nefāstum: nefāstus *dreadful*
certum: certus *certain, infallible*
vērī: vērus *true, real*
medicī: medicus *doctor*
mūrem: mūs *mouse*
nigrum: niger *black*
captum: captus *captured, caught*
dissecāre *cut up*
languidum: languidus *weak, feeble*
aurem: auris *ear*

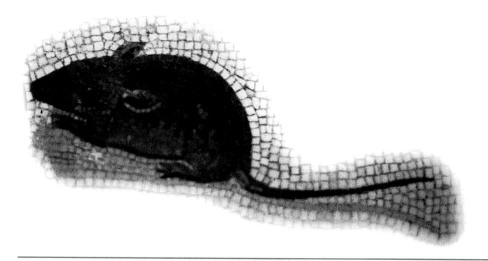

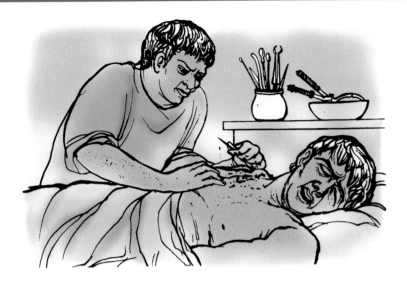

Petrō

Petrō, postquam dē vulnere Barbillī audīvit, statim ad vīllam
eius festīnāvit. ubi cubiculum intrāvit, astrologum vīdit, quī
Barbillum sānāre temptābat. astrologus mūrem dissectum in
vulnus dominī collocābat, versum magicum recitāns. Petrō,
simulac mūrem cōnspexit, īrātissimus erat; astrologum
verberāvit et ē cubiculō expulit.

    tum Petrō, postquam umerum Barbillī īnspexit, spongiam
cēpit et in acētō summersit. eam in vulnus collocāvit. Barbillus
exanimātus reccidit.

    Petrō ad mē sē vertit.

    "necesse est tibi mē adiuvāre," inquit. "difficile est mihi
Barbillum sānāre. dē vītā eius dēspērō, quod tam multus sanguis
etiam nunc effluit."

    itaque medicō auxilium dedī. Petrō, postquam aquam
ferventem postulāvit, manūs forcipemque dīligenter lāvit.
deinde, forcipem firmē tenēns, vulnus cum summā cūrā
īnspexit. postquam hoc cōnfēcit, umerum Barbillī lāvit; cutem,
quam hasta servī secuerat, perītē cōnseruit. dēnique umerum
firmē dēligāvit.

    mē ita monuit Petrō:

    "nunc necesse est Barbillō in hōc lectō manēre; necesse est eī
quiēscere et dormīre. nātūra sōla eum sānāre potest, nōn
astrologus."

    Petrōnī grātiās maximās ēgī. apud Barbillum diū manēbam,
negōtium eius administrāns. Barbillus enim mihi sōlī cōnfīdēbat.
cotīdiē ad cubiculum, ubi iacēbat aeger, veniēbam. multōs
sermōnēs cum Barbillō habēbam, prope lectum sedēns.
postquam Barbillum familiārissimē cognōvī, ille mihi dē vītā suā
multum nārrāvit. sine dubiō fortūna eum graviter afflīxerat.

	eius *his*
	dissectum: dissectus
	cut up, dismembered
5	**versum magicum: versus**
	magicus *magic spell*
	spongiam: spongia *sponge*
	acētō: acētum *vinegar*
	summersit: summergere *dip*
10	**reccidit: recidere** *fall back*
15	**ferventem: fervēns** *boiling*
	forcipem: forceps
	doctor's tongs, forceps
	firmē *firmly*
	cutem: cutis *skin*
20	**perītē** *skillfully*
	cōnseruit: cōnserere *stitch*
	monuit: monēre *advise*
	quiēscere *rest*
	nātūra *nature*
25	
	familiārissimē: familiāriter
	closely, intimately
	afflīxerat: afflīgere *afflict, hurt*

About the language 1: present participles

1 Study the following sentences:

medicus, per forum **ambulāns**, Phormiōnem cōnspexit.
*The doctor, **walking** through the forum, caught sight of Phormio.*

Clēmēns Eutychum in mediā viā **stantem** invēnit.
*Clemens found Eutychus **standing** in the middle of the road.*

Phormiō ancillās in cubiculō **lacrimantēs** audīvit.
*Phormio heard the slave girls **crying** in the bedroom.*

The words in **boldface** are present participles. A present participle is used to describe a noun. For example, in the first sentence, **ambulāns** describes the noun **medicus**.

2 Further examples:

  a astrologus in cubiculum irrūpit, clāmāns.
  b puerī, per urbem currentēs, Petrōnem cōnspexērunt.
  c spectātōrēs sacerdōtem ē templō discēdentem vīdērunt.
  d Galatēa iuvenēs in locō optimō stantēs vituperāvit.

Pick out the present participle in each sentence and find the noun it describes.

3 Study the different forms of the present participle (masculine and feminine):

SINGULAR

nominative	portāns	docēns	trahēns	audiēns
accusative	portantem	docentem	trahentem	audientem

PLURAL

nominative	portantēs	docentēs	trahentēs	audientēs
accusative	portantēs	docentēs	trahentēs	audientēs

4 Further examples:

  a fūr ē vīllā effūgit, cachinnāns.
  b rēx mīlitēs, prō templō sedentēs, spectābat.
  c Helena in hortō ambulābat, cantāns.
  d puellae, in pompā ambulantēs, rosās spargēbant.
  e Clēmēns fēlem sacram in tabernā iacentem invēnit.

Pick out the noun and participle pair in each sentence and state whether it is nominative or accusative, singular or plural.

fortūna crūdēlis

When you have read this story, answer the questions on page 139.

Barbillus uxōrem fidēlem fīliumque optimum habēbat. Plōtīna, uxor Barbillī, erat fēmina placida, quae domī manēbat contenta. Rūfus, fīlius eōrum, erat iuvenis impiger. ad palaestram cum amīcīs saepe adībat; in dēsertīs bēstiās ferōcēs agitāre solēbat. aliquandō, sīcut aliī iuvenēs, contentiōnēs cum parentibus habēbat. sed parentēs Rūfī eum maximē amābant, et ille eōs.

    inter amīcōs Rūfī erat iuvenis Athēniēnsis, Eupor. hic Eupor ad urbem Alexandrīam vēnerat et medicīnae studēbat. saepissimē domum Barbillī vīsitābat. tandem ad urbem Athēnās rediit, ubi artem medicīnae exercēbat. Eupor mox epistulam scrīpsit, in quā Rūfum parentēsque ad nūptiās suās invītāvit. Rūfus ad Graeciam īre valdē cupiēbat, sed Barbillus nāvigāre timēbat, quod hiems iam appropinquābat. astrologum suum igitur arcessīvit, et sententiam eius rogāvit. astrologus, postquam diū cōgitāvit, Rūfō parentibusque respōnsum dedit.

    "rem perīculōsam suscipitis. lūna Scorpiōnem iam intrat. tūtius est vōbīs domī manēre."

    Barbillus et uxor astrologō, quī erat vir doctissimus, libenter crēdidērunt, sed Rūfus rem graviter ferēbat. ubi Barbillus aberat, Rūfus saepe ad mātrem ībat, patrem dēplōrāns:

    "pater stultissimus est, quod astrologō crēdit. astrologī nōn sunt nautae. nihil dē arte nāvigandī sciunt."

placida: placidus *calm, peaceful*
domī *at home*
eōrum *their*
5 **impiger** *lively, energetic*
in dēsertīs *in the desert*
aliquandō *sometimes*
maximē *very much*
Athēniēnsis *Athenian*
10 **medicīnae: medicīna** *medicine*
studēbat: studēre *study*
artem: ars *art*
exercēbat: exercēre *practice*
nūptiās: nūptiae *wedding*
15 **respōnsum** *answer*
Scorpiōnem: Scorpiō
    Scorpio (sign of the zodiac)
tūtius est *it would be safer*

20

nāvigandī *of sailing*

itaque Rūfus Plōtīnae persuāsit, sed patrī persuādēre nōn
poterat. Barbillus obstinātus nāvigāre nōluit. Rūfus igitur et
Plōtīna Barbillum domī relīquērunt, et ad Graeciam nāvigābant.
ubi tamen nāvis, quae eōs vehēbat, Graeciae appropinquābat,
ingēns tempestās eam obruit. Rūfus ad lītus natāre poterat, sed
Plōtīna, quam Barbillus valdē amābat, in magnīs undīs periit.

ubi Barbillus dē naufragiō, in quō uxor perierat, audīvit,
maximē commōtus erat. fīlium iterum vidēre nōlēbat. Rūfus,
quamquam domum redīre volēbat, patrī pārēbat. in Graeciā diū
manēbat; sed tandem iter in Britanniam fēcit, ubi in exercitū
Rōmānō mīlitāvit.

25 relīquērunt: relinquere *leave*
    vehēbat: vehere *carry*
    tempestās *storm*
    obruit: obruere *overwhelm*

30 commōtus *upset, distressed*
    pārēbat: pārēre *obey*
    exercitū: exercitus *army*

Questions

1 What are we told about Plotina's character in lines 1–2? Give three details.
2 Why is **iuvenis impiger** (line 3) a good description of Rufus? Give two reasons for your answer.
3 What kind of a relationship did Rufus have with his parents (lines 5–6)?
4 What was Eupor doing in Alexandria?
5 When did Eupor write his letter? What did the letter contain (lines 9–11)?
6 Why did Barbillus ask for the opinion of his astrologer (lines 12–14)?
7 What was the astrologer's reply (lines 16–17)?
8 **Rūfus rem graviter ferēbat.** Why do you think Rufus was upset? What did he do (lines 19–20)?
9 In lines 23–24, to what extent did Rufus get his own way?
10 What happened when the ship was approaching Greece? What happened to Rufus and Plotina?
11 Why did Rufus not return home? What did he do after leaving Greece (lines 30–33)?
12 In line 21 Rufus said, "**pater stultissimus est, quod astrologō crēdit.**" From what happened to Barbillus and his family, do you think Rufus was right? Give a reason for your answer.

Plotina and Rufus would have sailed in a cargo ship like this one. There were no ships that carried only passengers in the Roman world.

About the language 2: *eum*, *eam*, etc.

1 You have now met various forms of the Latin word for "him," "her," "them," etc.:

	SINGULAR		PLURAL	
	masculine	*feminine*	*masculine*	*feminine*
genitive	eius	eius	eōrum	eārum
dative	eī	eī	eīs	eīs
accusative	eum	eam	eōs	eās

Clēmēns officīnam intrāvit. Eutychus **eum** salūtāvit.
Clemens entered the workshop. Eutychus greeted him.

servī ingentēs erant. Clēmēns tamen **eōs** neglēxit.
The slaves were huge. However, Clemens ignored them.

Barbillus mē ad cēnam invītāvit. ego ad vīllam **eius** contendī.
Barbillus invited me to dinner. I hurried to his house.

latrōnēs celeriter convēnērunt. Eutychus **eīs** fūstēs trādidit.
The thugs assembled quickly. Eutychus handed out clubs to them.

2 Further examples:

a Barbillus in cubiculō iacēbat. Quīntus eī vīnum dedit.
b Galatēa marītum vituperābat. tōta turba eam audīvit.
c puellae suāviter cantābant. Aristō vōcēs eārum laudāvit.
d ubi Petrō advēnit, Phormiō eum ad cubiculum dūxit.

For a complete chart of all forms, see page 166.

astrologus victor

I

astrologus, quī in vīllā Barbillī habitābat, erat vir ingeniī prāvī.   **vir ingeniī prāvī** *a man of evil*
astrologus et Petrō inimīcī erant. astrologus Syrius, medicus   *character*
Graecus erat. Petrō artem medicīnae in urbe diū exercuerat.
multī Alexandrīnī, quōs Petrō sānāverat, artem eius laudābant.
  astrologus tamen in vīllā Barbillī habitābat, Petrō in urbe   5
Alexandrīā. facile igitur erat astrologō Barbillum vīsitāre. ad
cubiculum, in quō dominus aeger iacēbat, saepe veniēbat. ubi
Petrō aberat, astrologus in aurem dominī dīcēbat,
  "in perīculō maximō es, domine. Petrō medicus pessimus est.
paucōs sānāvit. multōs aegrōs ad mortem mīsit. num Petrōnī   10

cōnfīdis? Petrō est vir avārissimus; nēmō est avārior quam ille. pecūniam tuam cupit. necesse est tibi eum ē vīllā expellere."

Barbillus astrologum anxius audīvit. sed, quamquam dolor cotīdiē ingravēscēbat, medicō etiam nunc crēdēbat. ubi medicum expellere Barbillus nōlēbat, astrologus cōnsilium cēpit. 15

dolor *pain*
ingravēscēbat: ingravēscere
grow worse

II

postrīdiē astrologus in cubiculum dominī irrūpit, clāmāns:

"domine! tibi nūntium optimum ferō. tē sānāre possum! dea Īsis, quae precēs meās semper audit, noctū somnium ad mē mīsit. in somniō per viās urbis Alexandrīae ambulābam. subitō puerum vīdī in viā stantem. puer erat servus tuus, quem 5 Aegyptiī in tumultū necāvērunt. mihi dē medicāmentō exquīsītissimō nārrāvit."

Barbillus, ubi hoc audīvit, astrologō sē tōtum trādidit. ille igitur, postquam medicāmentum composuit, umerum dominī aperuit et ūnxit. sed medicāmentum astrologī pessimum erat. 10 ingravēscēbat vulnus Barbillī.

astrologus, ubi hoc sēnsit, ē vīllā fūgit perterritus. Barbillus, dē vītā suā dēspērāns, mē ad cubiculum arcessīvit.

"mī Quīnte," inquit, in aurem susurrāns, "nōlī lacrimāre! moritūrus sum. id plānē intellegō. necesse est omnibus mortem 15 obīre. hoc ūnum ā tē postulō. fīlium meum in Britanniā quaere! refer eī hanc epistulam! ubi Rūfum ē vīllā expulī īrātus, eī magnam iniūriam intulī. nunc tandem veniam ā Rūfō petō."

ubi hoc audīvī, Petrōnem arcessere volēbam, sed Barbillus obstinātus recūsābat. arcessīvī tamen illum. sed ubi advēnit, 20 Barbillus iam mortuus erat.

nūntium: nūntius *news*
precēs *prayers*
noctū *by night*
somnium *dream*
medicāmentō: medicāmentum
ointment
exquīsītissimō: exquīsītus *special*
composuit: compōnere
put together, mix, make up
ūnxit: unguere *anoint, smear*

obīre *meet*
refer: referre *carry, deliver*
iniūriam intulī: iniūriam īnferre
do an injustice to,
bring injury to

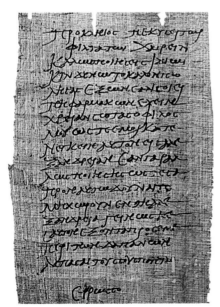

A letter from Alexandria, written in Greek on papyrus in the first century AD.

Practicing the language

1 Complete each sentence with the correct form of the participle. Then translate
the sentence.

    a Barbillus, dē vītā . . . ., Quīntum arcessīvit.
        (dēspērāns, dēspērantēs)

    b Quīntus lībertum in tabernā . . . . invēnit.
        (labōrāns, labōrantem)

    c sacerdōtēs, prō templō . . . ., silentium poposcērunt.
        (stāns, stantēs)

    d hippopotamum . . . . nōn cōnspexī.
        (adveniēns, advenientem)

    e Aegyptiī per viās cucurrērunt, magnum clāmōrem . . . .
        (tollēns, tollentēs)

    f Clēmēns tabernāriōs ā latrōnibus . . . . vīdit.
        (fugiēns, fugientēs)

    g puer mortuus dēcidit, dominum . . . .
        (dēfendēns, dēfendentem, dēfendentēs)

    h Aristō iuvenēs versum scurrīlem . . . . audīvit.
        (recitāns, recitantem, recitantēs)

2 Complete each sentence with the correct form of the verb. Then translate the sentence.

    a Barbillus: Quīnte! mēcum ad vēnātiōnem . . . .!
                     (venī, venīte)

    b Phormiō: servī! ad flūmen Nīlum . . . .!
                     (prōcēde, prōcēdite)

    c astrologus: domine! . . . . ē vīllā discēdere!
                     (nōlī, nōlīte)

    d Quīntus: amīce! nōlī astrologō . . . .!
                     (crēde, crēdere)

    e Phormiō: servī! ad mediam palūdem cautē . . . .!
                     (nāvigā, nāvigāte)

    f Barbillus: Aethiopes! hastās . . . .!
                     (ēmitte, ēmittite)

    g Quīntus: servī! . . . . hippopotamum vexāre!
                     (nōlī, nōlīte)

    h Barbillus: Quīnte! vulnerātus sum. mē . . . .!
                     (servā, servāte)

3 Translate into English:

Narcissus

Aristō: Galatēa! fortūna nōbīs favet! iuvenis Narcissus,
quem herī vīdimus, Helenae dōnum mīsit.
dōnum, quod iuvenis mīsit, pretiōsissimum est.
dōnum mihi quoque mīsit. iuvenis Narcissus
Helenam nostram amat.   5

Galatēa: quid dīcis, asine? iuvenis, quī prope nōs stābat,
fīliae nostrae dōnum mīsit? ēheu! marītum
stultissimum habeō. parentēs Narcissī humilēs
sunt. māter est Aegyptia, pater caupō. taberna,
quam tenet, sordida est.   10

humilēs: humilis *low-born, of low class*

Aristō: parentēs, quōs vituperās, nōn nōvī. sed
Narcissus ipse probus et benignus est. iuvenis
etiam līberālis est. libellum enim mihi dedit.
(*Aristō libellum īnspicit.*) ēheu! Narcissus poēta
est. suōs versūs scurrīlēs mihi mīsit.   15

libellum: libellus *little book*

Galatēa: fortūna nōbīs favet! nunc marītus meus illī
iuvenī Helenam dare nōn vult.

Write out the relative clauses in this story and state the
noun which each relative clause describes.

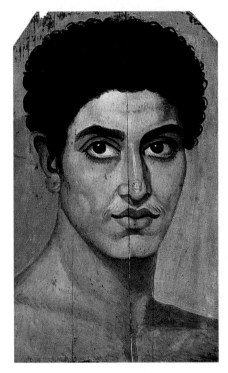

Narcissus

Medicine and science

Soon after its foundation, Alexandria became famous as a center of science and learning. The Museum and its Library, which were set up and financed by the Greek rulers of Egypt, attracted scholars from all over the Greek world, both to learn and to teach. They quickly began to make discoveries in all the sciences, including medicine. A good beginning had already been made in medicine by the Greek, Hippocrates, who had attempted to remove magic and superstition from the treatment of disease by observing his patients' symptoms carefully and trying to discover their causes. Hippocrates, who lived on the island of Cos in the fifth century BC, was rightly regarded as the founder of medical science. He and his followers pledged themselves to high standards of conduct in the famous Hippocratic oath. Part of it reads as follows:

> *Into whatever houses I enter, I will go into them for the benefit of the sick, and I will abstain from every voluntary act of mischief and corruption. Whatever in my professional practice I see or hear, which ought not to be spoken abroad, I will not divulge.*

However, Hippocrates and his Greek followers usually investigated only the surface of the body and not its interior; this was because the Greeks felt the idea of dissecting a body was disagreeable and perhaps wicked. The Egyptians, with a different attitude to the body, had gained a limited knowledge of anatomy from the dissection necessary for their ancient custom of mummifying corpses. Alexandria was therefore a

A sealstone carved with a picture of a doctor examining a patient, supervised by Aesculapius, the god of healing.

Alexandrian doctors were particularly expert about the inside of the body, although others had some knowledge. This clay model of the intestines, and models of other body parts, were dedicated to the gods by patients at a healing shrine in Italy.

A set of medical instruments carved on the walls of an Egyptian temple about twenty-five years after Quintus' visit to Alexandria. In the third row notice the scales for weighing medicines, and the forceps. The cups in the bottom left corner were used to draw off blood.

The bronze cup was heated and its mouth was applied to a patch of skin whose surface had been cut or scratched. As the air in the cup cooled, blood was gently sucked out.

A saw for cutting through bone.

A stamp for labeling cakes of eye ointment and a plaster cast of the impressions of the four sides.

During childbirth, the mother would sit in the birthing chair with female supporters around her and the midwife seated in front of her.

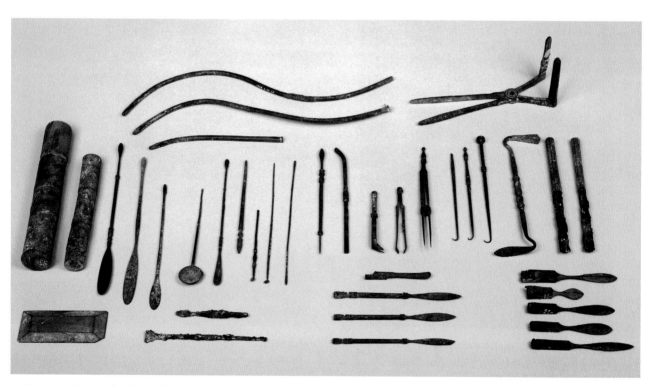

A Roman doctor had a wide range of instruments at his disposal.

good place for studying anatomy. Herophilus, the most famous Alexandrian anatomist, gave a detailed description of the brain, explained the differences between tendons and nerves, arteries and veins, and described the optic nerve and the eye, including the retina. He also measured the frequency of the pulse and used this to diagnose fever. Like earlier doctors, he laid great stress on the importance of hygiene, diet, exercise, and bathing.

In addition to general advice of this kind, an experienced doctor of the first century AD would treat minor ailments with drugs. The juice of the wild poppy, which contains opium, was used to relieve pain. Unwashed sheep's wool, containing lanolin, was often applied to wounds and swellings to soothe the irritation. Many prescriptions, however, would have been useless. For example, one account of the treatment of chilblains begins: "In the first place the chilblains are to be fomented thoroughly with boiled turnips. . ." Any benefit felt by the patient would be due not to the turnips, but to the heat of the fomentation or the patient's own belief that the treatment would do him or her good.

Some prescriptions are rather alarming, such as this for severe toothache: "When a tooth decays, there is no great need to remove it, but if the pain compels its removal, a peppercorn or an ivy berry should be inserted into the cavity of the tooth, which will then split and fall out in bits."

Minor surgery was regularly practiced: "Tonsils are covered by a thin layer of skin. If they become hardened after inflammation, they should be scratched round with a finger and drawn out. If they cannot be drawn out in this way they should be gripped with a hook and cut out with a scalpel. The

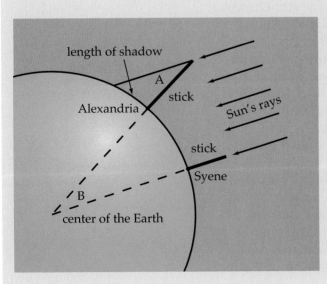

Diagram of Eratosthenes' experiment

Eratosthenes discovered that at Syene (modern Aswan) in southern Egypt the Sun was directly overhead at noon on the day of the summer solstice so that a vertical stick cast no shadow. At the same moment, the Sun in Alexandria (which Eratosthenes believed was due north of Syene) was not directly overhead, so that a stick in Alexandria did cast a shadow. Eratosthenes measured this shadow and used his measurement to calculate the angle A between the Sun's rays and the stick. Since the Sun's rays are parallel, angle B is the same size as angle A. Knowing angle B and the distance between Syene and Alexandria, he was able to calculate the circumference of the Earth.

Part of a papyrus treatise on astronomy, written in Greek at Alexandria in the second century BC.

hollow should then be swilled out with vinegar and the wound smeared with something to check the blood."

Fractures and wounds presented greater problems. Nevertheless, doctors were able to make incisions, tie veins and arteries, reset broken bones with splints, and stitch up wounds. Difficult or very delicate operations were sometimes attempted, such as operations on the eye to relieve cataracts. Amputation of limbs was undertaken only as a last resort.

Female patients could be tended by a minority of female doctors. Midwives were on hand to assist in one of the most important events in a Roman woman's life: childbirth. This was a dangerous time for both mother and child. The midwife's implements for easing labor pains and ensuring the safe delivery of the child included olive oil, herbs, sponges, woolen bandages, and a birthing stool.

Like Petro in the story on page 136, Greek doctors insisted on high standards of cleanliness in operations, to reduce the risk of infection. Although the quality of medical treatment in the ancient world would naturally vary considerably from one doctor to another, it is probably true that the standards of the best doctors were not improved upon in western Europe until about 150 years ago.

Hero's steam turbine.

The Museum at Alexandria was also famous for the study of mathematics. Euclid, who worked there in the third century BC, wrote a book known as the *Elements*, in which he summarized all previous knowledge of geometry; it continued to be used as a school textbook until relatively recent times. In applying their mathematical knowledge to the world around them, the Greeks at Alexandria reached some very accurate conclusions. For example, Eratosthenes calculated that the circumference of the Earth was 24,662 miles (39,459 kilometers); this is remarkably close to the true figure of 24,860 miles (40,008 kilometers).

Astronomy, which had begun in Babylonia, was developed further at Alexandria. Astronomers at Alexandria made the first attempts at calculating the distances between the Earth and the Sun, and between the Earth and the Moon. The ideas were also put forward that the Earth was round, rotated on its axis, and circled the Sun with the other planets. However, the heliocentric model of the universe found little favor among astronomers until Copernicus elaborated it in the 1500s. It is remarkable that Alexandrian astronomers devised their theories and made their calculations without the aid of telescopes or other accurate instruments.

Hero of Alexandria invented the first steam turbine, in the form of a toy, in which a hollow ball was mounted on two brackets on the lid of a vessel of boiling water. One bracket was hollow and conducted steam from the vessel into the ball. The steam escaped from the ball by means of two bent pipes, thus creating a force which made the ball spin around. He also made a hollow altar where, when a fire was lit, hot air streamed through four bent pipes to make puppets dance.

We also know of two female scholars from Alexandria. Mary the Jewess (Maria Hebraea) is said by some sources to have contributed to the study of alchemy by inventing several scientific instruments, including the double boiler ("bain-marie") for gentle heating. Hypatia of Alexandria wrote and taught about mathematics, philosophy, and astronomy. Among her achievements was, in collaboration with her father, a commentary on Euclid's *Elements*.

However, the Alexandrians did not take advantage of their scientific discoveries to build complicated and powerful machines for use in industry. Perhaps they felt they had no need for such machines, as they had a large workforce of slaves and free men; perhaps they regarded trade and manufacturing as less dignified than scientific research and investigation; or perhaps they were prevented from developing industrial machinery by their lack of technical skills such as the ability to make large metal containers and hold them together with screws and welds. Whatever the reason, some of the discoveries made by the Alexandrians were not put to industrial use until many centuries later.

Hypatia of Alexandria.

Vocabulary checklist 20

adeō, adīre, adiī	*go up to, approach*	**relinquō, relinquere, relīquī**	*leave*
arcessō, arcessere, arcessīvī	*summon, send for*	**sīcut**	*like*
		tam	*so*
ars, artis, f.	*art*	**temptō, temptāre, temptāvī**	*try*
crūdēlis	*cruel*	**vulnus, vulneris, n.**	*wound*
dēnique	*at last, finally*		
dēspērō, dēspērāre, dēspērāvī	*despair*	**ūnus**	*one*
doctus, docta, doctum	*learned, clever*	**duo**	*two*
domus, domūs, f.	*home*	**trēs**	*three*
īnferō, īnferre, intulī	*bring in, bring on*	**quattuor**	*four*
		quīnque	*five*
līberō, līberāre, līberāvī	*free, set free*	**sex**	*six*
lūna, lūnae, f.	*moon*	**septem**	*seven*
mors, mortis, f.	*death*	**octō**	*eight*
oculus, oculī, m.	*eye*	**novem**	*nine*
persuādeō, persuādēre, persuāsī	*persuade*	**decem**	*ten*
		vīgintī	*twenty*
pessimus, pessima, pessimum	*very bad, worst*	**trīgintā**	*thirty*
		quadrāgintā	*forty*
		quīnquāgintā	*fifty*

LANGUAGE INFORMATION

Contents

Part One: About the language
Nouns

1

	first declension	second declension		
gender	f.	m.	m.	n.
SINGULAR				
nominative and *vocative*	puella	servus (*voc.* serve)	faber	templum
genitive	puellae	servī	fabrī	templī
dative	puellae	servō	fabrō	templō
accusative	puellam	servum	fabrum	templum
ablative	puellā	servō	fabrō	templō
PLURAL				
nominative and *vocative*	puellae	servī	fabrī	templa
genitive	puellārum	servōrum	fabrōrum	templōrum
dative	puellīs	servīs	fabrīs	templīs
accusative	puellās	servōs	fabrōs	templa
ablative	puellīs	servīs	fabrīs	templīs

2 The vocative case is used when someone is being spoken to:

    ubi es, serve?   *Where are you, slave?*

3 Some 2nd declension nouns such as **faber** have a nominative and vocative singular ending in **-er**. All their other cases are formed like the cases of **servus**.

2nd declension nouns ending **-ius** drop the ending completely in the vocative (e.g. **fīlī**, **Salvī**).

4 The ablative case is used with certain prepositions:

    sacerdōs in templō stābat.   *The priest was standing in the temple.*

5 1st declension nouns like **puella** are usually feminine.

2nd declension nouns are usually either masculine like **servus**, or neuter like **templum**.

3rd declension nouns may be either masuline like **mercātor**, or feminine like **vōx**, or neuter like **nōmen**.

*third
declension*

m.	m.	f.	m. f.	n.	n.	*gender*
						SINGULAR
mercātor	leō	vōx	cīvis	nōmen	mare	*nominative* and *vocative*
mercātōris	leōnis	vōcis	cīvis	nōminis	maris	*genitive*
mercātōrī	leōnī	vōcī	cīvī	nōminī	marī	*dative*
mercātōrem	leōnem	vōcem	cīvem	nōmen	mare	*accusative*
mercātōre	leōne	vōce	cīve	nōmine	marī	*ablative*
						PLURAL
mercātōrēs	leōnēs	vōcēs	cīvēs	nōmina	maria	*nominative* and *vocative*
mercātōrum	leōnum	vōcum	cīvium	nōminum	marium	*genitive*
mercātōribus	leōnibus	vōcibus	cīvibus	nōminibus	maribus	*dative*
mercātōrēs	leōnēs	vōcēs	cīvēs	nōmina	maria	*accusative*
mercātōribus	leōnibus	vōcibus	cīvibus	nōminibus	maribus	*ablative*

6   Study the two nouns **templum** and **nōmen**. Notice that the forms **templum** and **nōmen** can be either nominative or accusative singular, and that **templa** and **nōmina** can be either nominative or accusative plural. That is because **templum** and **nōmen** are *neuter*. Every neuter noun uses the same form for both its nominative and accusative.

7   With the help of the noun tables find the Latin for the words in **boldface** in the following sentences:

   a We saw the **lion** in the wood.

   b The **girls** were reading in the garden.

   c The sound of their **voices** stopped Aristo writing.

   d Many **merchants** travelled to Britain.

   e The master gave a reward to his brave **slaves**.

   f The eruption terrified the **citizens**.

   g The **craftsman** carved a beautiful statue.

   h Do you like my **name**?

8 Study the following nouns:

gender	fourth declension		fifth declension	
	m.	f.	m.	f.
SINGULAR				
nominative and vocative	portus	manus	diēs	rēs
genitive	portūs	manūs	diēī	reī
dative	portuī	manuī	diēī	reī
accusative	portum	manum	diem	rem
ablative	portū	manū	diē	rē
PLURAL				
nominative and vocative	portūs	manūs	diēs	rēs
genitive	portuum	manuum	diērum	rērum
dative	portibus	manibus	diēbus	rēbus
accusative	portūs	manūs	diēs	rēs
ablative	portibus	manibus	diēbus	rēbus

9 **portus** and **manus** belong to the fourth declension, and **diēs** and **rēs** to the fifth. Compare their endings with those of the other declensions. Notice especially the form and pronunciation of the genitive singular, nominative plural, and accusative plural of **portus** and **manus**.

10 4th declension nouns like **portus** are usually masculine.

5th declension nouns like **rēs** are usually feminine.

11 With the help of the noun tables above, find the Latin for the words in **boldface** in the following sentences:

a Seven **days** had now passed.

b The **harbors** at Alexandria were huge.

c The priest raise his **hand**.

d The mother washed the child's **hands** and face.

e The messenger explained the **affair** to the slaves.

f It was the sixth hour of the **day**.

12 Translate the following sentences, which contain examples of the dative case. Be careful to distinguish between singular and plural forms.

   a Vārica dominō pecūniam trādidit.
   b rēx uxōrī dōnum comparāvit.
   c imperātor lībertīs et cīvibus spectāculum dedit.
   d Salvius vīlicō et agricolae canem ostendit.
   e puer iuvenibus et senī rem nārrāvit.
   f ancillae mercātōrī et mīlitibus triclīnium parāvērunt.
   g coquus dominō et amīcīs respondit.
   h nūntius cīvī et nautae crēdēbat.

13 The **genitive case** is introduced in Stage 17.

    puer ad tabernam **Clēmentis** cucurrit.
    *The boy ran to **Clemens'** shop.*

    spectātōrēs clāmābant, sed rēx clāmōrēs **spectātōrum** nōn audīvit.
    *The spectators were shouting, but the king did not hear the shouts **of the spectators**.*

    iuvenis vōcem **fēminae** laudāvit.
    *The young man praised the **woman's** voice.*

Further examples:

   a Quīntus, quī prope nāvem stābat, vōcēs nautārum audīvit.
   b Īsis erat dea Aegyptia. sacerdōtēs ad templum deae cotīdiē ībant.
   c magna multitūdō mīlitum in viā nōbīs obstābat.
   d clāmōrēs puerōrum senem vexābant.
   e prīncipēs ad aulam rēgis quam celerrimē contendērunt.
   f in vīllā amīcī meī saepe cēnābam.

14 Translate the following sentences which contain examples of the ablative case.

   a vīlla Barbillī longē ā portū abest.
   b fēlēs sub mēnsā sedēbat.
   c prō officīnā Eutychī stābant quattuor servī ingentēs.
   d Holcōnius dē hīs rēbus nihil cūrāvit.
   e aquila ex effigiē ēvolāvit.
   f Helena sine amīcīs ad vīllam revēnit.

Adjectives

1 In Stages 14 and 18 you have seen how an adjective changes its endings to agree with the noun it describes in three ways: case, number, and gender.

2 Most adjectives in Latin belong either to the 1st and 2nd declension or to the 3rd declension. The adjective **bonus** "good" is one that belongs to the 1st and 2nd declension:

	SINGULAR			PLURAL		
	masculine	*feminine*	*neuter*	*masculine*	*feminine*	*neuter*
nominative and *vocative*	bonus (voc. bone)	bona	bonum	bonī	bonae	bona
genitive	bonī	bonae	bonī	bonōrum	bonārum	bonōrum
dative	bonō	bonae	bonō	bonīs	bonīs	bonīs
accusative	bonum	bonam	bonum	bonōs	bonās	bona
ablative	bonō	bonā	bonō	bonīs	bonīs	bonīs

Compare the endings of **bonus** with those of the 1st and 2nd declension nouns **servus**, **puella**, and **templum** listed on page 154.

3 The adjective **fortis** "brave" is one that belongs to the 3rd declension:

	SINGULAR			PLURAL		
	masculine	*feminine*	*neuter*	*masculine*	*feminine*	*neuter*
nominative and *vocative*	fortis	fortis	forte	fortēs	fortēs	fortia
genitive	fortis	fortis	fortis	fortium	fortium	fortium
dative	fortī	fortī	fortī	fortibus	fortibus	fortibus
accusative	fortem	fortem	forte	fortēs	fortēs	fortia
ablative	fortī	fortī	fortī	fortibus	fortibus	fortibus

Compare the endings of **fortis** with those of the 3rd declension nouns **vōx**, **cīvis**, and **mare** listed on page 155.

4 With the help of paragraphs 2 and 3, find the correct form of **bonus** or **fortis** to agree with the noun in **boldface**, and then translate the sentences.

a mercātor **fīliam** . . . . laudāvit. (bonus)
b rēx **mīlitēs** . . . . salūtāvit. (fortis)
c **hominēs** . . . . dīligenter labōrābant. (bonus)
d scrībe librum dē . . . . **rēbus**! (bonus)
e **fēmina** . . . . latrōnī restitit. (fortis)
f dominus **puerīs** . . . . praemium dedit. (fortis)
g fabrī effigiem **imperātōris** . . . . fēcērunt. (bonus)
h prīnceps **cīvium** . . . . est vulnerātus. (fortis)
i pater **uxōrī** . . . . pecūniam dedit. (bonus)
j Quīntus **cōnsilia** . . . . cēpit. (bonus)

Comparatives and superlatives

1 In Stage 8, you met the **superlative** form of the adjective:

Clēmēns est **laetissimus**.   coquus est **stultissimus**.
*Clemens is **very happy**.*   *The cook is **very stupid**.*

2 In Stage 10, you met the **comparative** form:

gladiātor erat **fortior** quam leō.   estis **stultiōrēs** quam asinī!
*The gladiator was **braver** than the lion.*   *You are **more stupid** than donkeys!*

3 Study the way in which the comparative and superlative are formed:

		comparative	superlative
positive			
nominative	*accusative*		
longus	longum	longior	longissimus
long		*longer*	*very long*
pulcher	pulchrum	pulchrior	pulcherrimus
beautiful		*more beautiful*	*very beautiful*
fortis	fortem	fortior	fortissimus
brave		*braver*	*very brave*
ferōx	ferōcem	ferōcior	ferōcissimus
fierce		*more fierce*	*very fierce*
facilis	facilem	facilior	facillimus
easy		*easier*	*very easy*

4 The comparative and superlative forms change their endings in the usual way to indicate case, number, and gender:

nominative:	leō **saevissimus** intrāvit.
	*A **very savage** lion entered.*
accusative:	leōnem **saevissimum** interfēcī.
	*I killed a **very savage** lion.*
singular:	Dumnorix est **callidior** quam Belimicus.
	*Dumnorix is **cleverer** than Belimicus.*
plural:	Rēgnēnsēs sunt **callidiōrēs** quam Canticī.
	*The Regnenses are **cleverer** than the Cantici.*

masculine:	dominus meus est **īrātissimus**.
	*My master is **very angry**.*
feminine:	uxor mea est **īrātissima**.
	*My wife is **very angry**.*

5 Some important adjectives form their comparatives and superlatives in an irregular way:

bonus	melior	optimus
good	*better*	*very good, best*
malus	pēior	pessimus
bad	*worse*	*very bad, worst*
magnus	maior	maximus
big	*bigger*	*very big, biggest*
parvus	minor	minimus
small	*smaller*	*very small, smallest*

and

multus	plūs	plūrimus
much	*more*	*very much, most*

which becomes in the plural:

multī	plūrēs	plūrimī
many	*more*	*very many, most*

6 Further examples:

a leō erat maior quam Herculēs.
b Clēmēns plūrēs amīcōs quam Eutychus habēbat.
c Aristō erat poēta melior quam Barbillus.
d Quīntus numquam nāvēs minōrēs vīderat.

7 Translate each sentence, then change the adjective in **boldface** into the superlative form, and translate again.

For example: ātrium **magnum** erat.   This becomes: ātrium **maximum** erat.
  *The hall was **big**.*   *The hall was **very big**.*

a vīlicus puerōs **bonōs** laudāvit.
b **multī** cīvēs in flammīs periērunt.
c Quīntus servīs **malīs** auxilium nōn dedit.
d Herculēs erat **magnus**, et **magnum** fūstem habēbat.
e prīmō flammae erant **parvae**.

8 The Latin word **quam** may be written with a positive adjective, a comparative adjective, and a superlative adjective or adverb. Study these examples:

> **quam pulchra** est puella!
> *How beautiful the girl is!*

> vōs Rōmānī estis **Graeciōrēs quam** nōs Graecī.
> *You Romans are **more Greek than** we Greeks.*

> Pompēiānī ad templum **quam celerrimē** contendērunt.
> *The Pompeians hurried **as quickly as possible** to the temple.*

Translate the following sentences which contain these three uses of **quam**.

a necesse est mihi cubiculum quam pūrissimum facere.
b quam ēlegāns est cubiculum!
c cubiculum tuum ēlegantius est quam tablīnum meum.
d quam plūrimī Alexandrīnī pompam splendidam Īsidis spectāre volēbant.
e ego sum callidior quam frāter meus.
f ego ex urbe quam celerrimē discēdō.

9 Translate the first sentence of each pair. Complete the second sentence with the comparative and superlative of the adjective given in parentheses at the end of the sentence. Use the first sentence of each pair as a guide. Then translate.

a canis est stultissimus; canem stultiōrem numquam vīdī. (stultus)
Volūbilis est . . . .; servum . . . . numquam vīdī. (laetus)

b frāter meus est sapientior quam tū; sapientissimus est. (sapiēns)
Bregāns est . . . . quam Loquāx; . . . . est. (īnsolēns)

c mīlitēs sunt fortiōrēs quam cīvēs; fortissimī sunt. (fortis)
servī sunt . . . . quam lībertī; . . . . sunt. (trīstis)

d Melissa vōcem suāvissimam habēbat; vōcem suāviōrem numquam audīvī. (suāvis)
Caecilius servum . . . . habēbat; servum . . . . numquam vīdī. (malus)

Pronouns I: ego, tū, nōs, vōs, sē

1 In Units 1 and 2, you have met words for "I," "me," "you" (singular and plural), "we," "us," etc. These words belong to a group of words known as **personal pronouns**:

	First person		Second person	
	singular (I)	*plural (we)*	*singular (you)*	*plural (you)*
nominative	ego	nōs	tū	vōs
genitive	meī	nostrum	tuī	vestrum
dative	mihi	nōbīs	tibi	vōbīs
accusative	mē	nōs	tē	vōs
ablative	mē	nōbīs	tē	vōbīs

domina **tē** laudāvit.
The mistress praised you.

senex **mihi** illum equum dedit.
The old man gave that horse to me.

nōs Rōmānī sumus mīlitēs.
We Romans are soldiers.

dominus **vōs** īnspicere vult.
The master wants to inspect you.

2 You have also met the pronoun **sē**, meaning "himself," "herself," or "themselves." It has the same form for both singular and plural, and it has no nominative case.

	singular and plural
nominative	(no forms)
genitive	suī
dative	sibi
accusative	sē
ablative	sē

Dumnorix in ursam **sē** coniēcit.
Dumnorix hurled himself at the bear.

servī in ōrdinēs longōs **sē** īnstrūxērunt.
The slaves drew themselves up in long lines.

rēgīna **sē** interfēcit.
The queen killed herself.

mercātor **sibi** vīllam ēmit.
The merchant bought the house for himself.

3 Note the Latin for "with me," "with you," etc.:

Salvius **mēcum** ambulābat.   Rūfilla **tēcum** sedēbat.
*Salvius was walking **with me**.*   *Rufilla was sitting **with you**.*

rēx **nōbīscum** cēnābat.   iuvenēs **vōbīscum** pugnābant?
*The king was dining **with us**.*   *Were the young men fighting **with you**?*

Belimicus **sēcum** cōgitābat.
*Belimicus thought **to himself**.*

Compare this with the usual Latin way of saying "with":

rēx **cum Salviō** ambulābat.
*The king was walking **with Salvius**.*

mīlitēs **cum iuvenibus** pugnābant.
*The soldiers were fighting **with the young men**.*

4 Further examples:

  a   ego tibi pecūniam dedī.
  b   rēx nōs ad aulam invītāvit.
  c   Cogidubnus nōbīscum sedēbat.
  d   cūr mē vituperās?
  e   Galatēa Aristōnem vituperāvit, sē laudāvit.
  f   necesse est vōbīs mēcum venīre.
  g   vōs Quīntō crēditis, sed Salvius mihi crēdit.
  h   tē pūnīre possum, quod ego sum dominus.
  i   fābulam dē vōbīs nārrant.
  j   prīncipēs sermōnēs inter sē habēbant.

Pronouns II: hic, ille, is

1 In Stage 19, you met various forms of the word **hic** meaning "this" (plural "these"). This word belongs to a group of words known as **demonstrative pronouns**. Here is a complete list:

	SINGULAR				PLURAL		
	masculine	*feminine*	*neuter*		*masculine*	*feminine*	*neuter*
nominative	hic	haec	hoc		hī	hae	haec
genitive	huius	huius	huius		hōrum	hārum	hōrum
dative	huic	huic	huic		hīs	hīs	hīs
accusative	hunc	hanc	hoc		hōs	hās	haec
ablative	hōc	hāc	hōc		hīs	hīs	hīs

hae stolae sunt sordidae!　　　　quis **hoc** fēcit?
These dresses are dirty!　　　　*Who did **this**?*

2 You have also met various forms of the pronoun **ille** meaning "that" (plural "those"). Here is a complete list:

	SINGULAR				PLURAL		
	masculine	*feminine*	*neuter*		*masculine*	*feminine*	*neuter*
nominative	ille	illa	illud		illī	illae	illa
genitive	illīus	illīus	illīus		illōrum	illārum	illōrum
dative	illī	illī	illī		illīs	illīs	illīs
accusative	illum	illam	illud		illōs	illās	illa
ablative	illō	illā	illō		illīs	illīs	illīs

illa taberna nunc est mea.　　　　spectā **illud**!
That shop is now mine.　　　　*Look at **that**!*

3 In Stage 20, you met various forms of the word for "him," "her," and "them." Here is a complete list of the pronoun **is, ea, id** meaning "he," "she," "it" (plural "they"):

	SINGULAR			PLURAL		
	masculine	*feminine*	*neuter*	*masculine*	*feminine*	*neuter*
nominative	is	ea	id	eī	eae	ea
genitive	eius	eius	eius	eōrum	eārum	eōrum
dative	eī	eī	eī	eīs	eīs	eīs
accusative	eum	eam	id	eōs	eās	ea
ablative	eō	eā	eō	eīs	eīs	eīs

iuvenēs **eam** laudāvērunt.   ego ad vīllam **eius** contendī.
*The young men praised **her**.*   *I hurried to **his** house.*

dominus **eī** praemium dedit.   senex cum **eīs** pugnāvit.
*The master gave a reward **to him**.*   *The old man fought with **them**.*

4 The various forms of **hic** and **ille** can also be used to mean "he," "she," "it," or "they."

ille tamen nōn erat perterritus.   nēmō **hunc** in urbe vīdit.
***He**, however, was not terrified.*   *No one saw **him** in the city.*

5 The following sentences include the different pronouns described on pages 163–166.

a postquam senex hoc dīxit, Barbillus eum laudāvit.
b in palaestrā erant multī āthlētae, quī sē exercēbant.
c quamquam puellae prope mē stābant, eās vidēre nōn poteram.
d illud est vīnum, quod Cogidubnus ex Ītaliā importāvit.
e simulac mercātōrēs advēnērunt, Clēmēns eīs pecūniam trādidit.
f dā mihi illum fūstem!
g Vārica Bregantī plaustra dēmōnstrāvit. Bregāns illa ēmōvit.
h mīlitēs, quōs imperātor mīserat, nōbīscum sedēbant.
i remedia, quae astrologus composuit, erant pessima.
j Barbillus hās statuās sibi ēmit.
k rēgīna, quae tē honōrāvit, nōs vituperāvit.
l simulac latrō hanc tabernam intrāvit, vōcem eius audīvī.

Pronouns III: quī

1 In Stages 15 and 16, you met various forms of the **relative pronoun quī**, which is placed at the start of a relative clause and means "who," "which," etc. Here is a complete list:

	SINGULAR			PLURAL		
	masculine	*feminine*	*neuter*	*masculine*	*feminine*	*neuter*
nominative	quī	quae	quod	quī	quae	quae
genitive	cuius	cuius	cuius	quōrum	quārum	quōrum
dative	cui	cui	cui	quibus	quibus	quibus
accusative	quem	quam	quod	quōs	quās	quae
ablative	quō	quā	quō	quibus	quibus	quibus

ursa, **quam** Quīntus vulnerāvit, nunc mortua est.
*The bear **which** Quintus wounded is now dead.*

ubi est templum, **quod** Augustus Caesar aedificāvit?
*Where is the temple **which** Augustus Caesar built?*

in mediō ātriō stābant mīlitēs, **quī** rēgem custōdiēbant.
*In the middle of the hall stood the soldiers, **who** were guarding the king.*

The noun described by a relative clause is known as the **antecedent** of the relative pronoun. For example, in the first Latin sentence above, **ursa** is the antecedent of **quam**.

2 Translate the following sentences.

a flōrēs, quī in hortō erant, rēgem dēlectāvērunt.
b puer, quem Aegyptiī interfēcērunt, Quīntum fortiter dēfendēbat.
c fabrī, quōs rēx ex Ītaliā arcessīverat, effigiem Claudiī fēcērunt.
d cubiculum, quod Quīntus intrāvit, ēlegantissimum erat.
e aula, in quā Cogidubnus habitābat, erat prope mare.

In each sentence pick out the antecedent and the relative pronoun.

Verbs

	first conjugation	*second conjugation*	*third conjugation*	*fourth conjugation*
PRESENT TENSE	*I carry, you carry, etc.*	*I teach, you teach, etc.*	*I drag, you drag, etc.*	*I hear, you hear, etc.*
	portō	doceō	trahō	audiō
	portās	docēs	trahis	audīs
	portat	docet	trahit	audit
	portāmus	docēmus	trahimus	audīmus
	portātis	docētis	trahitis	audītis
	portant	docent	trahunt	audiunt
IMPERFECT TENSE	*I was carrying*	*I was teaching*	*I was dragging*	*I was hearing*
	portābam	docēbam	trahēbam	audiēbam
	portābās	docēbās	trahēbās	audiēbās
	portābat	docēbat	trahēbat	audiēbat
	portābāmus	docēbāmus	trahēbāmus	audiēbāmus
	portābātis	docēbātis	trahēbātis	audiēbātis
	portābant	docēbant	trahēbant	audiēbant
PERFECT TENSE	*I (have) carried*	*I (have) taught*	*I (have) dragged*	*I (have) heard*
	portāvī	docuī	trāxī	audīvī
	portāvistī	docuistī	trāxistī	audīvistī
	portāvit	docuit	trāxit	audīvit
	portāvimus	docuimus	trāximus	audīvimus
	portāvistis	docuistis	trāxistis	audīvistis
	portāvērunt	docuērunt	trāxērunt	audīvērunt
PLUPERFECT TENSE	*I had carried*	*I had taught*	*I had dragged*	*I had heard*
	portāveram	docueram	trāxeram	audīveram
	portāverās	docuerās	trāxerās	audīverās
	portāverat	docuerat	trāxerat	audīverat
	portāverāmus	docuerāmus	trāxerāmus	audīverāmus
	portāverātis	docuerātis	trāxerātis	audīverātis
	portāverant	docuerant	trāxerant	audīverant
INFINITIVE	*to carry*	*to teach*	*to drag*	*to hear*
	portāre	docēre	trahere	audīre
IMPERATIVE	*carry!*	*teach!*	*drag!*	*hear!*
	portā	docē	trahe	audī
	portāte	docēte	trahite	audīte

1 Translate the following examples:

portābant; portāvimus; trahēbās; trahitis;
docuērunt; audīvī; portābāmus; docuistī

2 Translate the following examples, then change them to mean "I..." instead of "he..." and translate again.

trahēbat; audīvit; docet;
intrāvit; dormiēbat; sedet

3 Translate the following examples, then change them from the plural to the singular, so that they mean "you (singular)..." instead of "they...," and translate again.

portāvērunt; trahunt; audīverant; manēbant; laudant; intellēxērunt

Persons and endings

1 The forms of the verb which indicate "I," "you" (singular), and "he" (or "she" or "it") are known as **1st**, **2nd**, and **3rd person singular**.
The forms which indicate "we," "you" (plural), and "they" are known as the **1st**, **2nd**, and **3rd person plural**.

The following table summarizes the Latin verb endings and the English translations which are used to indicate the different persons:

English		Latin verb ending	
		PRESENT IMPERFECT PLUPERFECT	PERFECT
I	1st person singular	-ō or -m	-ī
you	2nd person singular	-s	-istī
he, she, it	3rd person singular	-t	-it
we	1st person plural	-mus	-imus
you	2nd person plural	-tis	-istis
they	3rd person plural	-nt	-ērunt

So a word like **trāxerant** can be either translated (*they had dragged*) or described (3rd person plural pluperfect). Two further examples, **portāvī** and **docent**, are translated and described as follows:

portāvī	*I carried*	1st person singular perfect
docent	*they teach*	3rd person plural present

2 Describe and translate the following examples.

trāxī; audīs; portābāmus; docuerant; ambulāvistī; dīxerat

Irregular verbs

PRESENT TENSE	*I am*	*I am able*	*I want*	*I bring*
	sum	possum	volō	ferō
	es	potes	vīs	fers
	est	potest	vult	fert
	sumus	possumus	volumus	ferimus
	estis	potestis	vultis	fertis
	sunt	possunt	volunt	ferunt
IMPERFECT TENSE	*I was*	*I was able*	*I was wanting*	*I was bringing*
	eram	poteram	volēbam	ferēbam
	erās	poterās	volēbās	ferēbās
	erat	poterat	volēbat	ferēbat
	erāmus	poterāmus	volēbāmus	ferēbāmus
	erātis	poterātis	volēbātis	ferēbātis
	erant	poterant	volēbant	ferēbant
PERFECT TENSE	*I was (have been)*	*I have been able*	*I (have) wanted*	*I (have) brought*
	fuī	potuī	voluī	tulī
	fuistī	potuistī	voluistī	tulistī
	fuit	potuit	voluit	tulit
	fuimus	potuimus	voluimus	tulimus
	fuistis	potuistis	voluistis	tulistis
	fuērunt	potuērunt	voluērunt	tulērunt
PLUPERFECT TENSE	*I had been*	*I had been able*	*I had wanted*	*I had brought*
	fueram	potueram	volueram	tuleram
	fuerās	potuerās	voluerās	tulerās
	fuerat	potuerat	voluerat	tulerat
	fuerāmus	potuerāmus	voluerāmus	tulerāmus
	fuerātis	potuerātis	voluerātis	tulerātis
	fuerant	potuerant	voluerant	tulerant
INFINITIVE	*to be*	*to be able*	*to want*	*to bring*
	esse	posse	velle	ferre

1 Notice the difference between the present and perfect tenses of **ferō**:

    ferō *I bring*   **tulī** *I brought*

Compare this with the way the word "go" changes in English:

    I go, you go, etc.   *I went, you went, etc.*

2 The negative forms for the present tense of **volō** *I want* are formed in an irregular way. Compare the forms of **volō** *I want* with those of **nōlō** *I do not want*:

I want,	*I do not want,*
you want,	*you do not want,*
etc.	*etc.*
volō	nōlō
vīs	nōn vīs
vult	nōn vult
volumus	nōlumus
vultis	nōn vultis
volunt	nōlunt

In all other tenses, **nōlō** follows the same pattern as **volō**.

    For example, **volēbam**, **nōlēbam**.

3 The verbs **absum** (*I am absent*) and **adsum** (*I am present*) are formed by adding **ab** and **ad** to the forms of **sum**.

I am,	*I am present,*	*I am absent,*
you are, etc.	*you are present, etc.*	*you are absent, etc.*
sum	adsum	absum
es	ades	abes
est	adest	abest
sumus	adsumus	absumus
estis	adestis	abestis
sunt	adsunt	absunt

4 Translate the following examples.

es	ades	ferunt
poterāmus	aberant	voluistī
tulit	sumus	ferēbātis
vīs	aderātis	abesse

Verbs with the dative

1 In Unit 1, you met a number of verbs, such as **faveō** and **crēdō**, which are often used with a noun in the dative case. For example:

> mercātōrēs **Holcōniō** favēbant.
> *The merchants gave their support **to Holconius**.*
> or *The merchants supported Holconius.*

2 You have now met some other verbs which are used in the same way:

> turba **nōbīs** obstat.
> *The crowd is an obstacle **to us**.*
> or *The crowd is obstructing us.*

> Clēmēns **latrōnibus** resistēbat.
> *Clemens put up a resistance **to the thugs**.*
> or *Clemens resisted the thugs.*

3 Further examples:

a Barbillus Quīntō cōnfidēbat.
b mīlitibus resistere nōn potuimus.
c tandem fīlius mātrī persuāsit.
d sacerdōtēs lentē templō appropinquāvērunt.

Word order

The word order in the following sentences is very common:

1 clāmābant Rēgnēnsēs.
The Regnenses were shouting.

intrāvit Cogidubnus.
Cogidubnus entered.

Further examples:

a lacrimābant ancillae.
b labōrābat Clēmēns.

c dormiēbat rēx.
d rīdēbant puerī.

2 amīcum salūtāvit.
He greeted his friend.

ancillās laudāvimus.
We praised the slave girls.

Further examples:

a cēnam parābant.
b dominōs audīvimus.

c pecūniam invēnit.
d mātrem vīdistis?

The following word orders are also found.

3 discum petēbat āthlēta.
The athlete was looking for the discus.

nautās vituperābat Belimicus.
Belimicus was cursing the sailors.

Further examples:

a amphoram portābat vīlicus.
b vīnum bibēbant prīncipēs.

c gladiātōrēs laudāvit nūntius.
d rosās spargēbant puellae.

4 mercātōrem rēx dēcēpit.
The king deceived the merchant.

equum agricola vēndidit.
The farmer sold the horse.

Further examples:

a fēminās dominus spectābat.
b leōnem gladiātor interfēcit.

c poētās rēgīna honōrāvit.
d templum sacerdōs intrāvit.

5 The following examples include all the different sorts of word order used in paragraphs 1–4:

a surrēxērunt prīncipēs.
b togam gerēbat.
c multitūdinem incitābat senex.

d rēgem cīvēs vīdērunt.
e mē dēcēpistī.
f fīlium pater vituperābat.

6 The following examples each contain a noun in the dative case:

nūntiō epistulam dedī.　　　　　　amīcīs crēdēbat.
I gave a letter to the messenger.　*He believed his friends.*

Further examples:

a mercātōrī pecūniam reddidit.　　**c** dominō resistēbant.
b mīlitibus cibum parāvī.　　　　　**d** tibi faveō.

7 Note the position of **enim**, **igitur**, and **tamen** in the following sentences.

apud Barbillum diū manēbam, negōtium eius administrāns. Barbillus **enim** mihi sōlī cōnfīdēbat.
*I stayed a long time with Barbillus, handling his business. **For** Barbillus trusted only me.*

Salvius fundum īnspicere voluit. Vārica **igitur** eum per agrōs et aedificia dūxit.
*Salvius wanted to inspect the farm. Varica, **therefore**, led him through the fields and buildings.*

Belimicus **tamen**, quī saxa ignōrābat, cursum rēctum tenēbat.
***However**, Belimicus, who did not know about the rocks, held a straight course.*

Further examples:

a puer Aegyptius Quīntum dē viā perīculōsā monuit. Quīntus tamen Clēmentem vīsitāre volēbat.
b Cogidubnus Claudium quotannīs honōrat. rēx igitur multōs prīncipēs ad aulam invītāvit.
c Diogenēs nōbīs fūstēs trādidit. Aegyptiī enim casam oppugnābant.

Longer sentences I: with **postquam**, **simulac**, etc.

1 In Unit 1 you met sentences like this:

> Salvius, postquam fundum īnspexit, ad vīllam revēnit.
> *Salvius, after he inspected the farm, returned to the house.*

Or, in more natural English:
After Salvius inspected the farm, he returned to the house.

2 You also met sentences which are like the one above but also contain a noun in the dative case. For example:

> Rūfilla, postquam Salviō rem nārrāvit, exiit.
> *Rufilla, after she told the story to Salvius, went out.*

Or, in more natural English:
After Rufilla told Salvius the story, she went out.

3 Further examples:

a geminī, postquam coquō cibum trādidērunt, ē culīnā discessērunt.
b nūntius, postquam cīvibus spectāculum nūntiāvit, ad tabernam festīnāvit.
c rēx, postquam gladiātōrī pecūniam dedit, leōnem mortuum īnspexit.

4 You have now met sentences with **quamquam** and **simulac**. Study the following examples:

a Pompēius custōdēs interfēcit.
Pompeius killed the guards.
Pompēius, quamquam invītus erat, custōdēs interfēcit.
Pompeius, although he was unwilling, killed the guards.

> Or, in more natural English:
> *Although Pompeius was unwilling, he killed the guards.*

b puer ē triclīniō contendit.
The boy hurried out of the dining room.

simulac Salvius signum dedit, puer ē triclīniō contendit.
As soon as Salvius gave the signal, the boy hurried out of the dining room.

5 Further examples:

  a coquus fūrem cōnspexit.
    coquus, simulac vīllam intrāvit, fūrem cōnspexit.
  b Salvius nōn erat contentus.
    Salvius, quamquam servī dīligenter labōrābant, nōn erat contentus.
  c Quīntus "ecce!" clāmāvit.
    simulac nāvem vīdit, Quīntus "ecce!" clāmāvit.
  d nūntius ad templum cucurrit.
    nūntius, quamquam fessus erat, ad templum cucurrit.

6 The following examples are different types of longer sentences.
Translate them.

  a amīcī, simulac tabernam vīdērunt dīreptam, ad Clēmentem cucurrērunt.
  b ubi Salvius revēnit īrātus, Bregāns fūgit.
  c imperātor, postquam sacerdōtibus praemium dedit, ē templō exiit.
  d Clēmēns, quod Eutychus tabernae iam appropinquābat, amīcōs arcessīvit.

7 Complete each sentence with the most suitable group of words
from the box below, and then translate. Use each group of words
once only.

> ubi saxō appropinquant
> quamquam ancilla dīligenter labōrābat
> simulac sacerdōtēs ē cellā templī prōcessērunt
> postquam hospitī cubiculum ostendit
> ubi iuvenēs laetī ad theātrum contendērunt
> quod turbam īnfestam audīre poterat

  a . . . . , domina nōn erat contenta.
  b necesse est nautīs, ... , cursum tenēre rēctum.
  c puer timēbat ē casā exīre, ...
  d . . . . , tacuērunt omnēs.
  e māter, ... , cibum in culīnā gustāvit.
  e . . . . , senex in tablīnō manēbat occupātus.

Longer sentences II

1   You have met several examples of this kind of sentence:

Rēgnēnsēs erant laetī, Canticī miserī.
The Regnenses were happy, the Cantici were miserable.

Britannī cibum laudāvērunt, Rōmānī vīnum.
The Britons praised the food, the Romans praised the wine.

2   Further examples:

a   ūnus servus est fūr, cēterī innocentēs.
b   Canticī Belimicum spectābant, Rēgnēnsēs Dumnorigem.

3   The following examples are slightly different:

sacerdōs templum, poēta tabernam quaerēbat.
The priest was looking for a temple, the poet was looking for an inn.

iuvenis Aegyptius, senex Graecus erat.
The young man was Egyptian, the old man was Greek.

4   Further examples:

a   Clēmēns attonitus, Quīntus īrātus erat.
b   mercātor stolās, caupō vīnum vēndēbat.
c   puer ad hortum, ancillae ad ātrium ruērunt.
d   Galatēa deam, iuvenēs Helenam spectābant.

Part Two: Vocabulary

1 Nouns are listed in the following way:

the nominative case, e.g. **servus** (*slave*);
the genitive case, e.g. **servī** (*of a slave*); this is explained in Stage 17;
the gender of the noun (m. = masculine, f. = feminine, n. = neuter);
this is explained in Stage 18.

So, if the following forms are given:
pāx, pācis, f.   *peace*
pāx means *peace*, **pācis** means *of peace*, and the word is feminine.

2 The genitive case indicates the declension to which a noun belongs.

puellae	1st declension
servī	2nd declension
leōnis	3rd declension
portūs	4th declension
reī	5th declension

3 Find the meaning and the declension number for each of the following.

   a seges
   b effigiēs
   c scapha
   d tumultus
   e umerus

4 Find the meaning and the gender for each of the following words, some of which are in the nominative case and some in the genitive.

a taurus		**d** manūs		**g** tempestātis	
b hastae		**e** diēī		**h** praediī	
c flūminis		**f** dolor		**i** impetus	

5 Adjectives are listed in the following way:

1st and 2nd declension adjectives are listed with the masculine, feminine, and neuter forms of the nominative singular, e.g. **bonus, bona, bonum**.

3rd declension adjectives are also usually listed with the masculine, feminine, and neuter forms of the nominative singular, e.g.

trīstis, trīstis, trīste   *sad*

Sometimes the genitive singular (which is the same for all genders) is added to show the stem, e.g.

ferōx, ferōx, ferōx, *gen.* **ferōcis**

6 Verbs are usually listed in the following way:

parō, **parāre**, **parāvī**   *prepare*

The first form listed (**parō**) is the 1st person singular of the present tense (*I prepare*).
The second form (**parāre**) is the infinitive (*to prepare*).
The third form (**parāvī**) is the 1st person singular of the perfect tense (*I prepared*).

So, if the following forms are given:

āmittō, **āmittere**, **āmīsī**   *lose*

āmittō means *I lose*, **āmittere** means *to lose*, **āmīsī** means *I lost*.

7 The infinitive indicates the conjugation to which a verb belongs.

parāre	1st conjugation
docēre	2nd conjugation
trahere	3rd conjugation
audīre	4th conjugation

8 Give the meaning for each of the following.

   a susurrō; susurrāre; susurrāvī.
   b agō; agere; ēgī.
   c haereō; impedīre; importāvī; vibrāre; interfēcī.

9 Give the conjugation number and the meaning for each of the following.

   a rapiō; dēsiliō; inveniō; accipiō.
   b nāvigō; dēfendō; emō; rogō.
   c relinquere; rīdēre; movēre; cōnsūmere.

10 All words which are given in the **Vocabulary checklists** for Stages 1–20 are marked with the Stage in which they are given. For example:

16   **dēlectō**, **dēlectāre**, **dēlectāvī**   *delight, please*

This means that **dēlectō** appears as a Vocabulary checklist word in Stage 16.

a

17	ā, ab	*from; by*
10	abeō, abīre, abiī	*go away*
	abiciō, abicere, abiēcī	*throw away*
6	absum, abesse, āfuī	*be gone, be absent, be away*
	accidō, accidere, accidī	*happen*
10	accipiō, accipere, accēpī	*accept, take in, receive*
	accurrēns, accurrēns, accurrēns, *gen.* accurrentis	*running up*
	acētum, acētī, n.	*vinegar*
3	ad	*to*
20	adeō, adīre, adiī	*approach, go up to*
	adeō	*so much, so greatly*
	adest *see* adsum	
	adiuvō, adiuvāre, adiūvī	*help*
	administrāns, administrāns, administrāns, *gen.* administrantis	*managing*
	administrō, administrāre, administrāvī	*manage*
	admittō, admittere, admīsī	*admit, let in*
	adōrō, adōrāre, adōrāvī	*worship*
5	adsum, adesse, adfuī	*be here, be present*
	adveniēns, adveniēns, adveniēns, *gen.* advenientis	*arriving*
13	adveniō, advenīre, advēnī	*arrive*
13	aedificium, aedificiī, n.	*building*
16	aedificō, aedificāre, aedificāvī	*build*
13	aeger, aegra, aegrum	*sick, ill*
	Aegyptius, Aegyptia, Aegyptium	*Egyptian*
	Aegyptus, Aegyptī, f.	*Egypt*
	aēneus, aēnea, aēneum	*made of bronze*
	aequus, aequa, aequum	*fair*
	Aethiopes, Aethiopum, m.f.pl.	*Ethiopians*
	afflīgō, afflīgere, afflīxī	*afflict, hurt*
	ager, agrī, m.	*field*
	agilis, agilis, agile	*nimble, agile*
8	agitō, agitāre, agitāvī	*chase, hunt*
15	agmen, agminis, n.	*column (of people), procession*
9	agnōscō, agnōscere, agnōvī	*recognize*

	agnus, agnī, m.	*lamb*
4	agō, agere, ēgī	*do, act*
	age!	*come on!*
19	grātiās agere	*thank, give thanks*
	negōtium agere	*do business, work*
	quid agis?	*how are you?*
5	agricola, agricolae, m.	*farmer*
	Alexandrīnus, Alexandrīna, Alexandrīnum	*Alexandrian*
	aliquandō	*sometimes*
14	aliquid	*something*
15	alius, alia, aliud	*other, another*
13	alter, altera, alterum	*the other, the second*
	ambulāns, ambulāns, ambulāns, *gen.* ambulantis	*walking*
5	ambulō, ambulāre, ambulāvī	*walk*
	amīca, amīcae, f.	*friend*
	amīcē	*in a friendly way*
2	amīcus, amīcī, m.	*friend*
12	āmittō, āmittere, āmīsī	*lose*
19	amō, amāre, amāvī	*love, like*
	amphora, amphorae, f.	*wine jar*
	amulētum, amulētī, n.	*amulet, lucky charm*
2	ancilla, ancillae, f.	*slave girl, slave woman*
	animal, animālis, n.	*animal*
17	animus, animī, m.	*spirit, soul, mind*
	animum recipere	*recover consciousness*
	anteā	*before*
	antīquus, antīqua, antīquum	*old, ancient*
	anus, anūs, f.	*old woman*
	anxius, anxia, anxium	*anxious*
	aperiō, aperīre, aperuī	*open*
	appāreō, appārēre, appāruī	*appear*
17	appropinquō, appropinquāre, appropinquāvī	*approach, come near to*
14	apud	*among, at the house of*
15	aqua, aquae, f.	*water*
	aquila, aquilae, f.	*eagle*
17	āra, ārae, f.	*altar*
	arānea, arāneae, f.	*spider's web*
	arātor, arātōris, m.	*plowman*
	arca, arcae, f.	*strongbox, chest*
20	arcessō, arcessere, arcessīvī	*summon, send for*
	ardeō, ardēre, arsī	*burn, be on fire*

	ārea, āreae, f.	courtyard	
	argenteus, argentea, argenteum	made of silver	
	armārium, armāriī, n.	chest, cupboard	
20	ars, artis, f.	art, skill	
	ascendō, ascendere, ascendī	climb, rise	
	asinus, asinī, m.	ass, donkey	
	assiduē	continually	
	astrologus, astrologī, m.	astrologer	
	Athēnae, Athēnārum, f.pl.	Athens	
	Athēniēnsis	Athenian	
	āthlēta, āthlētae, m.	athlete	
	ātrium, ātriī, n.	atrium, reception hall	
14	attonitus, attonita, attonitum	astonished	
18	audeō, audēre	dare	
5	audiō, audīre, audīvī	hear, listen to	
14	aula, aulae, f.	palace	
	aurātus, aurāta, aurātum	gilded, gold-plated	
	aureus, aurea, aureum	golden, made of gold	
	aureus, aureī, m.	gold coin	
	auris, auris, f.	ear	
16	auxilium, auxiliī, n.	help	
	avārus, avāra, avārum	miserly, stingy	
	avārus, avārī, m.	miser	
	avidus, avida, avidum	eager	

b

	bālō, bālāre, bālāvī	bleat	
17	bene	well	
17	benignus, benigna, benignum	kind	
	bēstia, bēstiae, f.	wild animal, beast	
3	bibō, bibere, bibī	drink	
16	bonus, bona, bonum	good	
	Britannī, Britannōrum, m.pl.	Britons	
	Britannia, Britanniae, f.	Britain	
	Britannicus, Britannica, Britannicum	British	

c

	cachinnāns, cachinnāns, cachinnāns, gen. cachinnantis	laughing, cackling	
	cachinnō, cachinnāre, cachinnāvī	laugh, cackle, roar with laughter	

	cachinnus, cachinnī, m.	laughter	
	caedō, caedere, cecīdī	kill	
	caerimōnia, caerimōniae, f.	ceremony	
	calcō, calcāre, calcāvī	step on	
10	callidus, callida, callidum	clever, smart	
	candēlābrum, candēlābrī, n.	lampstand, candelabrum	
1	canis, canis, m.	dog	
	canistrum, canistrī, n.	basket	
	cantāns, cantāns, cantāns, gen. cantantis	singing, chanting	
13	cantō, cantāre, cantāvī	sing, chant	
	capillī, capillōrum, m.pl.	hair	
11	capiō, capere, cēpī	take, catch, capture	
	cōnsilium capere	make a plan, have an idea	
	captus, capta, captum	taken, caught, captured	
18	caput, capitis, n.	head	
	carnifex, carnificis, m.	executioner	
19	cārus, cāra, cārum	dear	
	casa, casae, f.	small house	
	caudex, caudicis, m.	blockhead, idiot	
	caupō, caupōnis, m.	innkeeper	
	cautē	cautiously	
	cecīdī see caedō		
	cēdō, cēdere, cessī	give in, yield	
	celebrō, celebrāre, celebrāvī	celebrate	
9	celeriter	quickly, fast	
	celerrimē	very quickly	
	quam celerrimē	as quickly as possible	
	cella, cellae, f.	sanctuary	
	cellārius, cellāriī, m.	(house) steward	
2	cēna, cēnae, f.	dinner	
7	cēnō, cēnāre, cēnāvī	eat dinner, dine	
	centum	a hundred	
	cēpī see capiō		
	cēra, cērae, f.	wax, wax tablet	
	cērātus, cērāta, cērātum	wax, made of wax	
	certāmen, certāminis, n.	struggle, contest	
	certāmen nāvāle	boat race	
	certō, certāre, certāvī	compete	
	certus, certa, certum	certain, infallible	
	cessī see cēdō		
13	cēterī, cēterae, cētera	the others, the rest	
2	cibus, cibī, m.	food	
	circum	around	

3	circumspectō, circumspectāre, circumspectāvī	look around	
	circumveniō, circumvenīre, circumvēnī,	surround	
	citharoedus, citharoedī, m.	cithara player	
11	cīvis, cīvis, m.f.	citizen	
	clādēs, clādis, f.	disaster	
	clam	secretly, in private	
	clāmāns, clāmāns, clāmāns, gen. clāmantis	shouting	
3	clāmō, clāmāre, clāmāvī	shout	
5	clāmor, clāmōris, m.	shout, uproar, racket	
	claudicō, claudicāre, claudicāvī	be lame, limp	
15	claudō, claudere, clausī	shut, close, block	
18	coepī	I began	
19	cōgitō, cōgitāre, cōgitāvī	think, consider	
18	cognōscō, cognōscere, cognōvī	get to know, find out	
	collēctus, collēcta, collēctum	gathered, assembled	
	colligō, colligere, collēgī	gather, collect, assemble	
	collocō, collocāre, collocāvī	place, put	
	columba, columbae, f.	dove, pigeon	
	cōmis, cōmis, cōme	polite, courteous, friendly	
	cōmiter	politely, courteously	
	commemorō, commemorāre, commemorāvī	talk about	
15	commodus, commoda, commodum	convenient	
	commōtus, commōta, commōtum	moved, upset, affected, alarmed, excited, distressed	
19	comparō, comparāre, comparāvī	obtain	
	competītor, competītōris, m.	competitor	
12	compleō, complēre, complēvī	fill	
	compōnō, compōnere, composuī	put together, arrange, mix, make up	
	condūcō, condūcere, condūxī	hire	
	cōnfectus, cōnfecta, cōnfectum	finished	
19	cōnficiō, cōnficere, cōnfēcī	finish	

	cōnfīdō, cōnfīdere	trust	
	coniciō, conicere, coniēcī	hurl, throw	
	coniungō, coniungere, coniūnxī	join	
	sē coniungere	join	
	coniūrātiō, coniūrātiōnis, f.	plot, conspiracy	
	coniūrō, coniūrāre, coniūrāvī	plot, conspire	
	cōnscendō, cōnscendere, cōnscendī	embark on, go on board	
	cōnscius, cōnsciī, m.	accomplice	
	cōnsecrō, cōnsecrāre, cōnsecrāvī	dedicate	
16	cōnsentiō, cōnsentīre, cōnsēnsī	agree	
	cōnserō, cōnserere, cōnseruī	stitch	
	cōnsīdō, cōnsīdere, cōnsēdī	sit down	
16	cōnsilium, cōnsiliī, n.	plan, idea	
	cōnsilium capere	make a plan, have an idea	
	cōnsistō, cōnsistere, cōnstitī	stand one's ground, stand firm	
7	cōnspiciō, cōnspicere, cōnspexī	catch sight of	
8	cōnsūmō, cōnsūmere, cōnsūmpsī	eat	
5	contendō, contendere, contendī	hurry	
	contentiō, contentiōnis, f.	argument	
10	contentus, contenta, contentum	satisfied	
	contrōversia, contrōversiae, f.	debate	
11	conveniō, convenīre, convēnī	come together, gather, meet	
	convertō, convertere, convertī	turn	
	sē convertere	turn	
4	coquō, coquere, coxī	cook	
1	coquus, coquī, m.	cook	
	corōna, corōnae, f.	garland, wreath, crown	
14	cotīdiē	every day	
11	crēdō, crēdere, crēdidī	trust, believe, have faith in	
	crīnēs, crīnium, m.pl.	hair	

	crocodīlus, crocodīlī, m.	crocodile
20	crūdēlis, crūdēlis, crūdēle	cruel
6	cubiculum, cubiculī, n.	bedroom
	cucurrī see currō	
	culīna, culīnae, f.	kitchen
7	cum	with
9	cupiō, cupere, cupīvī	want
4	cūr?	why?
	cūra, cūrae, f.	care
19	cūrō, cūrāre, cūrāvī	take care of, supervise
	nihil cūrō	I don't care
	currēns, currēns, currēns, gen. currentis	running
5	currō, currere, cucurrī	run
	cursus, cursūs, m.	course
12	custōdiō, custōdīre, custōdīvī	guard
13	custōs, custōdis, m.	guard
	cutis, cutis, f.	skin

d

	dare see dō	
11	dē	from, down from; about
18	dea, deae, f.	goddess
15	dēbeō, dēbēre, dēbuī	owe, ought, should, must
20	decem	ten
	dēcidō, dēcidere, dēcidī	fall down
	dēcipiō, dēcipere, dēcēpī	deceive, trick
14	decōrus, decōra, decōrum	right, proper
	dedī see dō	
	dēfendēns, dēfendēns, dēfendēns, gen. dēfendentis	defending
	dēfendō, dēfendere, dēfendī	defend
	dēiciō, dēicere, dēiēcī	throw down, throw
16	deinde	then
16	dēlectō, dēlectāre, dēlectāvī	delight, please
14	dēleō, dēlēre, dēlēvī	destroy
	dēliciae, dēliciārum, f.pl.	darling
	dēligātus, dēligāta, dēligātum	tied up, moored
	dēligō, dēligāre, dēligāvī	bind, tie, tie up
18	dēmōnstrō, dēmōnstrāre, dēmōnstrāvī	point out, show
	dēnārius, dēnāriī, m.	a denarius (small coin worth four sesterces)

20	dēnique	at last, finally
	dēpellō, dēpellere, dēpulī	drive off
	dēplōrāns, dēplōrāns, dēplōrāns, gen. dēplōrantis	complaining about
	dēplōrō, dēplōrāre, dēplōrāvī	complain about
	dērīdeō, dērīdēre, dērīsī	mock, make fun of
	dēscendō, dēscendere, dēscendī	come down
	dēserō, dēserere, dēseruī	desert
	dēsertus, dēserta, dēsertum	deserted
	in dēsertīs	in the desert
	dēsiliō, dēsilīre, dēsiluī	jump down
	dēspērāns, dēspērāns, dēspērāns, gen. dēspērantis	despairing
20	dēspērō, dēspērāre, dēspērāvī	despair
	dēstringō, dēstringere, dēstrīnxī	draw (a sword), pull out
14	deus, deī, m.	god
	dexter, dextra, dextrum	right
	ad dextram	to the right
	diadēma, diadēmatis, n.	diadem, crown
13	dīcō, dīcere, dīxī	say
	dictō, dictāre, dictāvī	dictate
9	diēs, diēī, m.	day
	diēs fēstus, diēī fēstī, m.	festival, holiday
14	difficilis, difficilis, difficile	difficult
	dignitās, dignitātis, f.	dignity
14	dīligenter	carefully, hard
	dīmittō, dīmittere, dīmīsī	send away, dismiss
	dīreptus, dīrepta, dīreptum	torn apart, ransacked
	dīrigō, dīrigere, dīrēxī	steer
	dīripiō, dīripere, dīripuī	tear apart, ransack
	dīrus, dīra, dīrum	dreadful, awful
	discēdēns, discēdēns, discēdēns, gen. discēdentis	leaving, departing
18	discēdō, discēdere, discessī	depart, leave
	discus, discī, m.	discus
	dissecō, dissecāre, dissecuī	cut up
	dissectus, dissecta, dissectum	cut up, dismembered
17	diū	for a long time
	diūtius	any longer, for too long

dīves, dīves, dīves,
   gen. dīvitis   *rich*
dīxī *see* dīcō

9 dō, dare, dedī   *give*

doceō, docēre, docuī   *teach*

20 doctus, docta, doctum   *educated, learned,*
        skillful, clever

dolor, dolōris, m.   *pain*

14 domina, dominae, f.   *lady (of the house),*
        mistress

2 dominus, dominī, m.   *master (of the house)*

20 domus, domūs, f.   *home*
   domī   *at home*
   domum redīre   *return home*

14 dōnum, dōnī, n.   *present, gift*

2 dormiō, dormīre,
   dormīvī   *sleep*

dubitō, dubitāre, dubitāvī   *be doubtful*

dubium, dubiī, n.   *doubt*

8 dūcō, dūcere, dūxī   *lead*

dulcis, dulcis, dulce   *sweet*
   mī dulcissime!   *my very dear friend!*

20 duo, duae, duo   *two*

dūrus, dūra, dūrum   *hard, harsh*

e

4 ē, ex   *from, out of*

eam   *her, it*

eārum   *their*

eās   *them*

3 ecce!   *see! look!*

effigiēs, effigiēī, f.   *image, statue*

effluō, effluere, efflūxī   *pour out, flow out*

effodiō, effodere, effōdī   *dig*

effringō, effringere, effrēgī   *break down*

16 effugiō, effugere, effūgī   *escape*

effundō, effundere, effūdī   *pour out*

ēgī *see* agō

4 ego, meī   *I, me*
   mēcum   *with me*

ehem!   *well, well!*

4 ēheu!   *alas! oh dear!*

eī   *to him, to her, to it*

eīs   *to them, for them*

eius   *his, her, its*

ēlegāns, ēlegāns,
   ēlegāns, *gen.* ēlegantis   *tasteful, elegant*

ēligō, ēligere, ēlēgī   *choose*

ēlūdō, ēlūdere, ēlūsī   *slip past*

9 ēmittō, ēmittere, ēmīsī   *throw, send out*

6 emō, emere, ēmī   *buy*

ēmoveō, ēmovēre, ēmōvī   *move, clear away*

enim   *for*

eō   *it*

11 eō, īre, iī   *go*

eōrum   *their*

eōs   *them*

12 epistula, epistulae, f.   *letter*

eques, *gen.* equitis, m.   *horseman*

equitō, equitāre, equitāvī   *ride (a horse)*

15 equus, equī, m.   *horse*

eram *see* sum

ērubēscēns, ērubēscēns,
   ērubēscēns, *gen.*
   ērubēscentis   *blushing*

ērumpō, ērumpere, ērūpī   *break away*

est *see* sum

3 et   *and*

15 etiam   *even, also*

euge!   *hurray!*

8 eum   *him*

ēvellēns, ēvellēns,
   ēvellēns, *gen.* ēvellentis   *wrenching off*

ēvertō, ēvertere, ēvertī   *overturn*

ēvolō, ēvolāre, ēvolāvī   *fly out*

ēvulsus, ēvulsa, ēvulsum   *wrenched off*

4 ex, ē   *from, out of*

exanimātus, exanimāta,
   exanimātum   *unconscious*

13 excitō, excitāre, excitāvī   *arouse, wake up*

exclāmāns, exclāmāns,
   exclāmāns, *gen.*
   exclāmantis   *exclaiming, shouting*

10 exclāmō, exclāmāre,
   exclāmāvī   *exclaim, shout*

3 exeō, exīre, exiī   *go out*

exerceō, exercēre, exercuī   *exercise*

exercitus, exercitūs, m.   *army*

expellō, expellere, expulī   *throw out*

exquīsītus, exquīsīta,
   exquīsītum   *special*

exspectātus, exspectāta,
exspectātum — *welcome*

3 exspectō, exspectāre,
exspectāvī — *wait for*

extendō, extendere, extendī — *stretch out*

extorqueō, extorquēre,
extorsī — *extort*

extrā — *outside*

extrahō, extrahere, extrāxī — *pull out, take out*

f

17 faber, fabrī, m. — *craftsman*
5 fābula, fābulae, f. — *play, story*
8 facile — *easily*
17 facilis, facilis, facile — *easy*
7 faciō, facere, fēcī — *make, do*

familiāris, familiāris, m. — *relation, relative*

familiāriter — *closely, intimately*

11 faveō, favēre, fāvī — *favor, support*

fax, facis, f. — *torch*

fēcī *see* faciō

fēlēs, fēlis, f. — *cat*

5 fēmina, fēminae, f. — *woman*

fenestra, fenestrae, f. — *window*

9 ferō, ferre, tulī — *bring, carry*

graviter ferre — *take badly*

6 ferōciter — *fiercely*

8 ferōx, ferōx,
ferōx, *gen.* ferōcis — *fierce, ferocious*

ferrum, ferrī, n. — *iron*

fervēns, fervēns,
fervēns, *gen.* ferventis — *boiling*

13 fessus, fessa, fessum — *tired*

6 festīnō, festīnāre, festīnāvī — *hurry*

fēstus, fēsta, fēstum — *festive, holiday*

diēs fēstus, diēī fēstī, m. — *festival, holiday*

14 fidēlis, fidēlis, fidēle — *faithful, loyal*

1 filia, fīliae, f. — *daughter*

1 filius, fīliī, m. — *son*

firmē — *firmly*

12 flamma, flammae, f. — *flame*

16 flōs, flōris, m. — *flower*

flūmen, flūminis, n. — *river*

19 fluō, fluere, flūxī — *flow*

foedus, foeda, foedum — *foul, horrible*

fōns, fontis, m. — *fountain*

forceps, forcipis, m. — *doctor's tongs, forceps*
18 fortasse — *perhaps*
19 forte — *by chance*
6 fortis, fortis, forte — *brave, strong*
12 fortiter — *bravely*

fortitūdō, fortitūdinis, f. — *courage*

fortūna, fortūnae, f. — *fortune, luck*

forum, forī, n. — *forum, business center*

fossa, fossae, f. — *ditch*

frāctus, frācta, frāctum — *broken*

frangēns, frangēns,
frangēns, *gen.* frangentis — *breaking*

10 frāter, frātris, m. — *brother*

frequentō, frequentāre,
frequentāvī — *crowd, fill*

frūmentum, frūmentī, n. — *grain*

12 frūstrā — *in vain*

fugiēns, fugiēns,
fugiēns, *gen.* fugientis — *running away, fleeing*

12 fugiō, fugere, fūgī — *run away, flee (from)*

fuī *see* sum

fundō, fundere, fūdī — *pour*

12 fundus, fundī, m. — *farm*

6 fūr, fūris, m. — *thief*

furēns, furēns,
furēns, *gen.* furentis — *furious, in a rage*

fūstis, fūstis, m. — *club, stick*

g

garriēns, garriēns,
garriēns, *gen.* garrientis — *chattering, gossiping*

garriō, garrīre, garrīvī — *chatter, gossip*

garum, garī, n. — *sauce*

geminī, geminōrum, m.pl. — *twins*

gemitus, gemitūs, m. — *groan*

gēns, gentis, f. — *family, tribe*

Germānicus, Germānica,
Germānicum — *German*

gerō, gerere, gessī — *wear*

gladiātor, gladiātōris, m. — *gladiator*

8 gladius, gladiī, m. — *sword*

Graecia, Graeciae, f. — *Greece*

Graecus, Graeca, Graecum — *Greek*

grātiae, grātiārum, f.pl. — *thanks*

19 grātiās agere — *thank, give thanks*

gravis, gravis, grave — *heavy*

17	graviter		*seriously*
	graviter ferre		*take badly*
	gustō, gustāre, gustāvī		*taste*

h

4	habeō, habēre, habuī	*have*
10	habitō, habitāre, habitāvī	*live*
	hāc	*this*
	hae	*these*
	haec	*this*
	haedus, haedī, m.	*kid, young goat*
	haereō, haerēre, haesī	*stick, cling*
	hanc	*this*
	hās	*these*
19	hasta, hastae, f.	*spear*
	hauriō, haurīre, hausī	*drain, drink up*
	hercle!	*by Hercules! good heavens*
7	heri	*yesterday*
	heus!	*hey!*
	hī	*these*
	hīs	*these*
8	hic	*this*
	hiemō, hiemāre, hiemāvī	*spend the winter*
	hiems, hiemis, f.	*winter*
	hippopotamus, hippopotamī, m.	*hippopotamus*
	hoc	*this*
	hōc	*this*
5	hodiē	*today*
9	homō, hominis, m.	*person, man*
	homunculus, homunculī, m.	*little man*
	honōrō, honōrāre, honōrāvī	*honor*
	hōra, hōrae, f.	*hour*
	horreum, horreī, n.	*barn, granary*
1	hortus, hortī, m.	*garden*
	hōs	*these*
9	hospes, hospitis, m.	*guest, host*
17	hūc	*here, to this place*
	humilis, humilis, humile	*low-born, of low class*
	hunc	*this*

i

| | iacēns, iacēns, iacēns, *gen.* iacentis | *lying, resting* |
| 12 | iaceō, iacēre, iacuī | *lie, rest* |

	iactō, iactāre, iactāvī	*throw*
12	iam	*now, already*
3	iānua, iānuae, f.	*door*
	ībam *see* eō	
18	ibi	*there*
	id	*it*
12	igitur	*therefore, and so*
8	ignāvus, ignāva, ignāvum	*lazy, cowardly*
	ignōrō, ignōrāre, ignōrāvī	*not know about*
	illa	*that, she*
	illā	*that*
	illae	*those*
	illam	*that*
	illās	*those*
9	ille	*that, he*
	illī	*they, those, that*
	illōs	*those*
19	illūc	*there, to that place*
	illud	*that*
	illum	*that*
	immemor, immemor immemor, *gen.* immemoris	*forgetful*
	immortālis, immortālis, immortāle	*immortal*
	immōtus, immōta, immōtum	*still, motionless*
	impavidus, impavida, impavidum	*fearless*
15	impediō, impedīre, impedīvī	*delay, hinder*
	impellō, impellere, impulī	*carry, push, force*
16	imperātor, imperātōris, m.	*emperor*
	impetus, impetūs, m.	*attack*
	impiger, impigra, impigrum	*lively, energetic*
	importō, importāre, importāvī	*import*
	impulī *see* impellō	
1	in (+ ABL)	*in, on*
	in (+ ACC)	*into, onto*
	incendēns, incendēns, incendēns, *gen.* incendentis	*burning, setting on fire*
	incitō, incitāre, incitāvī	*urge on, encourage*
	incolumis, incolumis, incolume	*safe*
	incurrō, incurrere, incurrī	*run onto, collide*
	inēlegāns, inēlegāns, inēlegāns, *gen.* inēlegantis	*unattractive*

	īnfēlīx, īnfēlīx, īnfēlīx, *gen.* īnfēlīcis	*unlucky*
20	īnferō, īnferre, intulī	*bring in, bring on*
	iniūriam īnferre	*do an injustice, bring injury*
	vim īnferre	*use force, violence*
	īnfestus, īnfesta, īnfestum	*hostile*
	īnfirmus, īnfirma, īnfirmum	*weak*
	īnflō, īnflāre, īnflāvī	*blow*
	ingenium, ingeniī, n.	*character*
7	ingēns, ingēns, ingēns, *gen.* ingentis	*huge*
	ingravēscō, ingravēscere	*grow worse*
	iniciō, inicere, iniēcī	*throw in*
	inimīcus, inimīcī, m.	*enemy*
	iniūria, iniūriae, f.	*injustice, injury*
	iniūstē	*unfairly*
	innocēns, innocēns, innocēns, *gen.* innocentis	*innocent*
4	inquit	*says, said*
	īnsānus, īnsāna, īnsānum	*insane, crazy*
	īnsiliō, īnsilīre, īnsiluī	*jump onto, jump into*
	īnsolēns, īnsolēns, īnsolēns, *gen.* īnsolentis	*rude, insolent*
9	īnspiciō, īnspicere, īnspexī	*look at, inspect, examine*
	īnstruō, īnstruere, īnstrūxī	*draw up*
	sē īnstruere	*draw oneself up*
17	īnsula, īnsulae, f.	*island*
7	intellegō, intellegere, intellēxī	*understand*
6	intentē	*intently*
16	inter	*among, between*
	inter sē	*among themselves, with each other*
	intereā	*meanwhile*
13	interficiō, interficere, interfēcī	*kill*
	interpellō, interpellāre, interpellāvī	*interrupt*
	interrogō, interrogāre, interrogāvī	*question*
2	intrō, intrāre, intrāvī	*enter*
	intulī *see* īnferō	
	inūtilis, inūtilis, inūtile	*useless*
10	inveniō, invenīre, invēnī	*find*
11	invītō, invītāre, invītāvī	*invite*
17	invītus, invīta, invītum	*unwilling, reluctant*
	iocus, iocī, m.	*joke*

14	ipsa	*herself*
14	ipse	*himself*
3	īrātus, īrāta, īrātum	*angry*
	īre *see* eō	
	irrumpō, irrumpere, irrūpī	*burst in*
	Īsiacus, Īsiacī, m.	*follower of Isis*
	ista	*that*
	istam	*that*
14	iste	*that*
	istum	*that*
16	ita	*in this way*
13	ita vērō	*yes*
	Ītalia, Ītaliae, f.	*Italy*
17	itaque	*and so*
19	iter, itineris, n.	*journey, progress*
9	iterum	*again*
	Iūdaeī, Iūdaeōrum, m.pl.	*Jews*
5	iuvenis, iuvenis, m.	*young man*

1

	labōrāns, labōrāns, labōrāns, *gen.* labōrantis	*working*
1	labōrō, labōrāre, labōrāvī	*work*
	lacrima, lacrimae, f.	*tear*
	lacrimīs sē trādere	*burst into tears*
	lacrimāns, lacrimāns, lacrimāns, *gen.* lacrimantis	*crying, weeping*
7	lacrimō, lacrimāre, lacrimāvī	*cry, weep*
	laedō, laedere, laesī	*harm*
2	laetus, laeta, laetum	*happy*
	languidus, languida, languidum	*weak, feeble*
	lateō, latēre, latuī	*lie hidden*
	lātrō, lātrāre, lātrāvī	*bark*
	latrō, latrōnis, m.	*robber, thug*
2	laudō, laudāre, laudāvī	*praise*
	lavō, lavāre, lāvī	*wash*
15	lectus, lectī, m.	*couch, bed*
11	legō, legere, lēgī	*read*
	lēniter	*gently*
15	lentē	*slowly*
3	leō, leōnis, m.	*lion*
	levis, levis, leve	*changeable, inconsistent*
	libellus, libellī, m.	*little book*
18	libenter	*gladly*
10	liber, librī, m.	*book*
11	līberālis, līberālis, līberāle	*generous*

20	līberō, līberāre, līberāvī	*free, set free*	
6	lībertus, lībertī, m.	*freedman, ex-slave*	
	lībō, lībāre, lībāvī	*pour an offering*	
	liquō, liquāre, liquāvī	*melt*	
15	lītus, lītoris, n.	*seashore, shore*	
19	locus, locī, m.	*place*	
	Londinium, Londiniī, n.	*London*	
	longē	*far, a long way*	
	longius	*further*	
	longus, longa, longum	*long*	
	loquāx, loquāx, loquāx, gen. loquācis	*talkative*	
	lucrum, lucrī, n.	*profit*	
	lūdus, lūdī, m.	*game*	
	lūdī fūnebrēs	*funeral games*	
20	lūna, lūnae, f.	*moon*	

m

	madidus, madida, madidum	*soaked through*
	magicus, magica, magicum	*magic*
	magis	*more*
	multō magis	*much more*
	magister, magistrī, m.	*foreman*
	magnificus, magnifica, magnificum	*splendid, magnificent*
3	magnus, magna, magnum	*big, large, great*
	maior, maior, maius, gen. maiōris	*bigger, larger, greater*
19	māne	*in the morning*
9	maneō, manēre, mānsī	*remain, stay*
	mānsuētus, mānsuēta, mānsuētum	*tame*
18	manus, manūs, f.	*hand*
15	mare, maris, n.	*sea*
14	marītus, marītī, m.	*husband*
	marmoreus, marmorea, marmoreum	*made of marble*
1	māter, mātris, f.	*mother*
	mātrōna, mātrōnae, f.	*lady*
	maximē	*most of all, very much*
17	maximus, maxima, maximum	*very big, very large, very great*
	mē *see* ego	
	medicāmentum, medicāmentī, n.	*ointment*
	medicīna, medicīnae, f.	*medicine*

	medicus, medicī, m.	*doctor*
9	medius, media, medium	*middle*
	mel, mellis, n.	*honey*
16	melior, melior, melius	*better*
	melius est	*it would be better*
	mendācior, mendācior, mendācior, gen. mendāciōris	*more deceitful*
4	mendāx, mendācis, m.	*liar*
	mēnsa, mēnsae, f.	*table*
	mēnsis, mēnsis, m.	*month*
2	mercātor, mercātōris, m.	*merchant*
	mēta, mētae, f.	*turning point*
	metallum, metallī, n.	*a mine*
5	meus, mea, meum	*my, mine*
	mī dulcissime!	*my very dear friend!*
	mī Salvī!	*my dear Salvius!*
	mihi *see* ego	
18	mīles, mīlitis, m.	*soldier*
	mīlitō, mīlitāre, mīlitāvī	*be a soldier*
11	minimē!	*no!*
12	mīrābilis, mīrābilis, mīrābile	*marvelous, strange, wonderful*
	mīrāculum, mīrāculī, n.	*miracle*
15	miser, misera, miserum	*miserable, wretched, sad*
	o mē miserum!	*oh wretched me!*
12	mittō, mittere, mīsī	*send*
	modicus, modica, modicum	*ordinary, little*
	molestus, molesta, molestum	*troublesome*
	moneō, monēre, monuī	*warn, advise*
12	mōns, montis, m.	*mountain*
	monumentum, monumentī, n.	*monument*
	moritūrus, moritūra, moritūrum	*going to die*
20	mors, mortis, f.	*death*
7	mortuus, mortua, mortuum	*dead*
	moveō, movēre, mōvī	*move*
9	mox	*soon*
	mulceō, mulcēre, mulsī	*pet, pat*
	multitūdō, multitūdinis, f.	*crowd*
5	multus, multa, multum	*much*
5	multī, multae, multa	*many*
	multō magis	*much more*

11	mūrus, mūrī, m.	*wall*
	mūs, mūris, m.f.	*mouse*
	mystēria, mystēriōrum, n.pl.	*mysteries, secret worship*

n

18	nam	*for*
7	nārrō, nārrāre, nārrāvī	*tell, relate*
	natō, natāre, natāvī	*swim*
	nātūra, nātūrae, f.	*nature*
	naufragium, naufragiī, n.	*shipwreck*
	naufragus, naufragī, m.	*shipwrecked sailor*
15	nauta, nautae, m.	*sailor*
16	nāvigō, nāvigāre, nāvigāvī	*sail*
3	nāvis, nāvis, f.	*ship*
	Neāpolis, Neāpolis, f.	*Naples*
14	necesse	*necessary*
7	necō, necāre, necāvī	*kill*
	nefāstus, nefāsta, nefāstum	*dreadful*
	neglegēns, neglegēns, neglegēns, *gen.* neglegentis	*careless*
	neglegō, neglegere, neglēxī	*ignore*
17	negōtium, negōtiī, n.	*business*
	negōtium agere	*do business, work*
18	nēmō	*no one, nobody*
	neque … neque	*neither … nor*
	niger, nigra, nigrum	*black*
7	nihil	*nothing*
	nihil cūrō	*I don't care*
	Nīlus, Nīlī, m.	*the river Nile*
	nitidus, nitida, nitidum	*gleaming, brilliant*
	niveus, nivea, niveum	*snow-white*
	nōbilis, nōbilis, nōbile	*noble, of noble birth*
	nōbīs *see* nōs	
	nocēns, nocēns, nocēns, *gen.* nocentis	*guilty*
	noceō, nocēre, nocuī	*hurt*
	noctū	*by night*
13	nōlō, nōlle, nōluī	*not want, be unwilling, refuse*
	nōlī	*do not, don't*
	nōmen, nōminis, n.	*name*
3	nōn	*not*
16	nōnne?	*surely?*

	nōnnūllī, nōnnūllae, nōnnūlla	*some, several*
10	nōs	*we, us*
	nōbīscum	*with us*
11	noster, nostra, nostrum	*our*
	nōtus, nōta, nōtum	*well-known, famous*
20	novem	*nine*
19	nōvī	*I know*
13	novus, nova, novum	*new*
13	nūllus, nūlla, nūllum	*not any, no*
14	num?	*surely … not?*
	numerō, numerāre, numerāvī	*count*
	numerus, numerī, m.	*number*
17	numquam	*never*
11	nunc	*now*
10	nūntiō, nūntiāre, nūntiāvī	*announce*
8	nūntius, nūntiī, m.	*messenger, news*
	nūper	*recently*
	nūptiae, nūptiārum, f.pl.	*wedding*

o

	obdormiō, obdormīre, obdormīvī	*fall asleep*
	obeō, obīre, obiī	*meet*
	obruō, obruere, obruī	*overwhelm*
	obstinātus, obstināta, obstinātum	*stubborn*
18	obstō, obstāre, obstitī	*obstruct, block the way*
	obtulī *see* offerō	
	occupātus, occupāta, occupātum	*busy*
20	oculus, oculī, m.	*eye*
	offendō, offendere, offendī	*displease*
9	offerō, offerre, obtulī	*offer*
	officīna, officīnae, f.	*workshop*
7	omnis, omnis, omne	*all*
	opportūnē	*just at the right time*
	oppugnō, oppugnāre, oppugnāvī	*attack*
12	optimē	*very well*
5	optimus, optima, optimum	*very good, excellent, best*
	ōrdō, ōrdinis, m.	*row, line*
	ōrnāmentum, ōrnāmentī, n.	*ornament*

ōrnātrīx, ōrnātrīcis, f.	hairdresser	
ōrnātus, ōrnāta, ōrnātum	decorated, elaborately furnished	
ōrnō, ōrnāre, ōrnāvī	decorate	
ōsculum, ōsculī, n.	kiss	
9 ostendō, ostendere, ostendī	show	
ostrea, ostreae, f.	oyster	
ōtiōsus, ōtiōsa, ōtiōsum	on holiday, idle, taking time off	
ōvum, ōvī, n.	egg	

P

12 paene	nearly, almost
palaestra, palaestrae, f.	palaestra, exercise ground
palūs, palūdis, f.	marsh, swamp
parātus, parāta, parātum	ready, prepared
parēns, parentis, m.f.	parent
pāreō, pārēre, pāruī	obey
7 parō, parāre, parāvī	prepare
18 pars, partis, f.	part
in prīmā parte	in the forefront
6 parvus, parva, parvum	small
1 pater, patris, m.	father
patera, paterae, f.	bowl
17 paucī, paucae, pauca	few, a few
paulātim	gradually
paulum, paulī, n.	little, a little
pavīmentum, pavīmentī, n.	floor
4 pecūnia, pecūniae, f.	money
6 per	through, along
percutiō, percutere, percussī	strike
16 pereō, perīre, periī	die, perish
perīculōsus, perīculōsa, perīculōsum	dangerous
19 perīculum, perīculī, n.	danger
perītē	skillfully
perītia, perītiae, f.	skill
perītus, perīta, perītum	skillful
20 persuādeō, persuādēre, persuāsī	persuade
4 perterritus, perterrita, perterritum	terrified

17 perveniō, pervenīre, pervēnī	reach, arrive at
8 pēs, pedis, m.	foot, paw
20 pessimus, pessima, pessimum	very bad, worst
pestis, pestis, f.	pest, rascal
5, 18 petō, petere, petīvī	head for, attack; seek, beg for, ask for
pharus, pharī, m.	lighthouse
philosophus, philosophī, m.	philosopher
pictor, pictōris, m.	painter, artist
pictūra, pictūrae, f.	painting, picture
pila, pilae, f.	ball
pingō, pingere, pīnxī	paint
pius, pia, pium	respectful to the gods
11 placeō, placēre, placuī	please, suit
placidus, placida, placidum	calm, peaceful
plānē	clearly
5 plaudō, plaudere, plausī	applaud, clap
plaustrum, plaustrī, n.	wagon, cart
plēnus, plēna, plēnum	full
pluit, pluere, pluit	rain
plūrimus, plūrima, plūrimum	very much, most
19 plūrimī, plūrimae, plūrima	very many
poena, poenae, f.	punishment
poenās dare	pay the penalty, be punished
4 poēta, poētae, m.	poet
pompa, pompae, f.	procession
Pompēiānus, Pompēiāna, Pompēiānum	Pompeian
16 pōnō, pōnere, posuī	place, put, put up
portāns, portāns, portāns, gen. portantis	carrying
3 portō, portāre, portāvī	carry
10 portus, portūs, m.	harbor
19 poscō, poscere, poposcī	demand, ask for
possideō, possidēre, possēdī	possess
13 possum, posse, potuī	can, be able
9 post	after, behind
18 posteā	afterwards
6 postquam	after, when
postrēmō	finally, lastly
16 postrīdiē	(on) the next day

8	postulō, postulāre, postulāvī	demand	
	posuī *see* pōnō		
	potuī *see* possum		
	praeceps, praeceps, praeceps, *gen.* praecipitis	straight for, headlong	
	praecursor, praecursōris, m.	forerunner	
	praedium, praediī, n.	estate	
	praemium, praemiī, n.	profit, prize, reward	
	praesidium, praesidiī, n.	protection	
	praesum, praeesse, praefuī	be in charge of	
	praetereō, praeterīre, praeteriī	go past	
	prāvus, prāva, prāvum	evil	
	precēs, precum, f.pl.	prayers	
	premō, premere, pressī	push	
	pretiōsus, pretiōsa, pretiōsum	expensive, precious	
	pretium, pretiī, n.	price	
	prīmō	first	
11	prīmus, prīma, prīmum	first	
	in prīmā parte	in the forefront	
15	prīnceps, prīncipis, m.	chief, chieftain	
	prior	first, in front	
18	prō	in front of	
	prō dī immortālēs!	heavens above!	
	probus, proba, probum	honest	
9	prōcēdō, prōcēdere, prōcessī	advance, proceed	
	procul	far off	
	prōcumbō, prōcumbere, prōcubuī	fall, fall down	
7	prope	near	
	prōvideō, prōvidēre, prōvīdī	foresee	
	proximus, proxima, proximum	nearest	
	psittacus, psittacī, m.	parrot	
5	puella, puellae, f.	girl	
8	puer, puerī, m.	boy	
	pugiō, pugiōnis, m.	dagger	
8	pugnō, pugnāre, pugnāvī	fight	
9	pulcher, pulchra, pulchrum	beautiful	

6	pulsō, pulsāre, pulsāvī	hit, knock on, whack, punch
	pūmiliō, pūmiliōnis, m.f.	dwarf
16	pūniō, pūnīre, pūnīvī	punish
	pūrus, pūra, pūrum	clean, spotless
	puto, putāre, putāvī	think, consider

q

	quā	which
	quae	who, which
	quaerēns, quaerēns, quaerēns, *gen.* quaerentis	searching for, looking for
4	quaerō, quaerere, quaesīvī	search for, look for, inquire
14	quam	(1) how
	quam celerrimē	as quickly as possible
10	quam	(2) than
	quam	(3) whom, which
14	quamquam	although
	quārtus, quārta, quārtum	fourth
	quās	whom, which
20	quattuor	four
14	-que	and
	quem	whom, which
15	quī	who, which
	quid?	what?
	quid agis?	how are you?
	quid vīs?	what do you want?
	quīdam	one, a certain
	quiēscō, quiēscere, quiēvī	rest
	quiētus, quiēta, quiētum	quiet
20	quīnque	five
4	quis?	who?
18	quō?	(1) where? where to?
	quō	(2) from whom
	quō modō?	how?
6	quod	(1) because
	quod	(2) which
17	quondam	one day, once
2	quoque	also, too
	quōs	whom, which
	quotannīs	every year

r

rādō, rādere, rāsī — scratch
rapiō, rapere, rapuī — seize, grab
rārō — rarely
raucus, rauca, raucum — harsh
recidō, recidere, reccidī — fall back
17 recipiō, recipere, recēpī — recover, take back
   sē recipere — recover
recitāns, recitāns, recitāns, *gen.* recitantis — reciting
recitō, recitāre, recitāvī — recite
rēctā — directly, straight
rēctus, rēcta, rēctum — straight
recumbēns, recumbēns, recumbēns, *gen.* recumbentis — lying down, reclining
recumbō, recumbere, recubuī — lie down, recline
18 recūsō, recūsāre, recūsāvī — refuse
4 reddō, reddere, reddidī — give back
15 redeō, redīre, rediī — return, go back, come back
referō, referre, rettulī — carry, deliver
reficiō, reficere, refēcī — repair
rēgīna, rēgīnae, f. — queen
20 relinquō, relinquere, relīquī — leave
remedium, remediī, n. — cure
renovō, renovāre, renovāvī — restore
6 rēs, reī, f. — thing, affair
   rem cōnficere — finish the job
   rem intellegere — understand the truth
   rem nārrāre — tell the story
   rēs rūstica — the farming
17 resistō, resistere, restitī — resist
3 respondeō, respondēre, respondī — reply
respōnsum, respōnsī, n. — answer
retineō, retinēre, retinuī — keep, hold back
retrahō, retrahere, retrāxī — drag back
9 reveniō, revenīre, revēnī — come back, return
14 rēx, rēgis, m. — king
rīdēns, rīdēns, rīdēns, *gen.* rīdentis — laughing, smiling
3 rīdeō, rīdēre, rīsī — laugh, smile
rīpa, rīpae, f. — river bank

7 rogō, rogāre, rogāvī — ask
rogus, rogī, m. — pyre
Rōmānus, Rōmāna, Rōmānum — Roman
rosa, rosae, f. — rose
rota, rotae, f. — wheel
13 ruō, ruere, ruī — rush
rūsticus, rūstica, rūsticum — country, in the country
   rēs rūstica — the farming
   vīlla rūstica — country house

s

sacer, sacra, sacrum — sacred
15 sacerdōs, sacerdōtis, m. — priest
sacrificium, sacrificiī, n. — offering, sacrifice
sacrificō, sacrificāre, sacrificāvī — sacrifice
8 saepe — often
saeviō, saevīre, saeviī — be in a rage
saevus, saeva, saevum — savage
saltātrīx, saltātrīcis, f. — dancing girl
saltō, saltāre, saltāvī — dance
2 salūtō, salūtāre, salūtāvī — greet
3 salvē! — hello!
sānē — obviously
8 sanguis, sanguinis, m. — blood
sānō, sānāre, sānāvī — heal, cure
sapiēns, sapiēns, sapiēns, *gen.* sapientis — wise
saxum, saxī, n. — rock
scapha, scaphae, f. — punt, small boat
scelestus, scelesta, scelestum — wicked
scēptrum, scēptrī, n. — scepter
scindō, scindere, scidī — tear, tear up
scio, scīre, scīvī — know
scōpae, scōpārum, f.pl. — broom
scopulus, scopulī, m. — reef
6 scrībō, scrībere, scrīpsī — write
scrīptor, scrīptōris, m. — writer
scurrīlis, scurrīlis, scurrīle — obscene, dirty
13 sē — himself, herself, themselves
   sēcum — with him, to himself
secō, secāre, secuī — cut

	secundus, secunda, secundum	*second*	
	sēcūrus, sēcūra, sēcūrum	*without a care*	
4	sed	*but*	
	sedēns, sedēns, sedēns, *gen.* sedentis	*sitting*	
1	sedeō, sedēre, sēdī	*sit*	
	seges, segetis, f.	*crop, harvest*	
	sella, sellae, f.	*chair*	
	sēmirutus, sēmiruta, sēmirutum	*half-collapsed*	
10	semper	*always*	
5	senex, senis, m.	*old man*	
	sententia, sententiae, f.	*opinion*	
12	sentiō, sentīre, sēnsī	*feel, notice*	
20	septem	*seven*	
	sermō, sermōnis, m.	*conversation*	
10	servō, servāre, servāvī	*save, protect*	
1	servus, servī, m.	*slave*	
	sibi	*to him (self), to her (self), to them (selves)*	
20	sīcut	*like*	
4	signum, signī, n.	*sign, seal, signal*	
	silentium, silentiī, n.	*silence*	
8	silva, silvae, f.	*woods, forest*	
16	simulac, simulatque	*as soon as*	
	sine	*without*	
	situs, sitūs, m.	*position, site*	
	sōl, sōlis, m.	*sun*	
18	soleō, solēre	*be accustomed, usually*	
	sollemniter	*solemnly*	
	sollicitūdō, sollicitūdinis, f.	*anxiety*	
11	sollicitus, sollicita, sollicitum	*worried, anxious*	
10	sōlus, sōla, sōlum	*alone, lonely, only, on one's own*	
	somnium, somniī, n.	*dream*	
	sonitus, sonitūs, m.	*sound*	
	sonō, sonāre, sonuī	*sound*	
	sonus, sonī, m.	*sound*	
	sordidus, sordida, sordidum	*dirty*	
	soror, sorōris, f.	*sister*	
	spargō, spargere, sparsī	*scatter*	

8	spectāculum, spectāculī, n.	*show, spectacle*	
	spectātor, spectātōris, m.	*spectator*	
5	spectō, spectāre, spectāvī	*look at, watch*	
	splendidus, splendida, splendidum	*splendid*	
	spongia, spongiae, f.	*sponge*	
	stāns, stāns, stāns, *gen.* stantis	*standing*	
8	statim	*at once*	
	statua, statuae, f.	*statue*	
	stilus, stilī, m.	*pen, stick*	
5	stō, stāre, stetī	*stand*	
	stola, stolae, f.	*(long) dress*	
	studeō, studēre, studuī	*study*	
11	stultus, stulta, stultum	*stupid, foolish*	
	suāvis, suāvis, suāve	*sweet*	
	suāviter	*sweetly*	
	sub	*under*	
6	subitō	*suddenly*	
	sūdō, sūdāre, sūdāvī	*sweat*	
	sufficiō, sufficere, suffēcī	*be enough*	
1	sum, esse, fuī	*be*	
	summergō, summergere, summersī	*sink, dip*	
	summersus, summersa, summersum	*sunk*	
16	summus, summa, summum	*highest, greatest, top*	
	superbus, superba, superbum	*arrogant, proud*	
6	superō, superāre, superāvī	*overcome, overpower, overtake*	
	supersum, superesse, superfuī	*survive*	
	supplicium, suppliciī, n.	*death penalty*	
	surdus, surda, surdum	*deaf*	
3	surgō, surgere, surrēxī	*get up, stand up, rise*	
	suscipiō, suscipere, suscēpī	*undertake, take on*	
	sustulī *see* tollō		
	susurrāns, susurrāns, susurrāns, *gen.* susurrantis	*whispering, mumbling*	
	susurrō, susurrāre, susurrāvī	*whisper, mumble*	

10	suus, sua, suum	*his (own), her (own), their (own)*	
	Syrī, Syrōrum, m.pl.	*Syrians*	
	Syrius, Syria, Syrium	*Syrian*	

t

3	taberna, tabernae, f.	*store, shop, inn*
	tabernārius, tabernāriī, m.	*storekeeper, shopkeeper*
	tablīnum, tablīnī, n.	*study*
10	taceō, tacēre, tacuī	*be silent, be quiet*
	tacitus, tacita, tacitum	*quiet, silent, in silence*
20	tam	*so*
7	tamen	*however*
12	tandem	*at last*
	tangō, tangere, tetigī	*touch*
	tantus, tanta, tantum	*so great, such a great*
	tardus, tarda, tardum	*late*
	taurus, taurī, m.	*bull*
	tē *see* tū	
	tempestās, tempestātis, f.	*storm*
12	templum, templī, n.	*temple*
20	temptō, temptāre, temptāvī	*try*
	tenēns, tenēns, tenēns, *gen.* tenentis	*holding, owning*
15	teneō, tenēre, tenuī	*hold, own*
	tergeō, tergēre, tersī	*wipe*
12	terra, terrae, f.	*ground, land*
7	terreō, terrēre, terruī	*frighten*
	terribilis, terribilis, terribile	*terrible*
	theātrum, theātrī, n.	*theater*
	tibi *see* tū	
	tībīcen, tībīcinis, m.	*pipe player*
12	timeō, timēre, timuī	*be afraid, fear*
	timidus, timida, timidum	*fearful, frightened*
	toga, togae, f.	*toga*
	tollēns, tollēns, tollēns, *gen.* tollentis	*raising, lifting up*
16	tollō, tollere, sustulī	*raise, lift up, hold up*
19	tot	*so many*
8	tōtus, tōta, tōtum	*whole*
	tractō, tractāre, tractāvī	*handle*
9	trādō, trādere, trādidī	*hand over*
	lacrimīs sē trādere	*burst into tears*

	tragoedia, tragoediae, f.	*tragedy*
13	trahō, trahere, trāxī	*drag*
	tranquillitās, tranquillitātis, f.	*calmness*
	trānsfīgō, trānsfīgere, trānsfīxī	*pierce*
20	trēs	*three*
	triclīnium, triclīniī, n.	*dining room*
20	trigintā	*thirty*
	tripodes, tripodum, m.pl. (acc. pl.: tripodas)	*tripods*
	trīstis, trīstis, trīste	*sad*
	trūdō, trūdere, trūsī	*push, shove*
4	tū, tuī	*you (singular)*
	tēcum	*with you (singular)*
	tuba, tubae, f.	*trumpet*
	tubicen, tubicinis, m.	*trumpeter*
	tulī *see* ferō	
6	tum	*then*
	tumultus, tumultūs, m.	*riot*
	tunica, tunicae, f.	*tunic*
5	turba, turbae, f.	*crowd*
	turbulentus, turbulenta, turbulentum	*rowdy, disorderly*
	tūtus, tūta, tūtum	*safe*
	tūtius est	*it would be safer*
6	tuus, tua, tuum	*your, yours*

u

5, 14	ubi	*where, when*
	ultor, ultōris, m.	*avenger*
	umerus, umerī, m.	*shoulder*
15	unda, undae, f.	*wave*
	unde	*from where*
	unguō, unguere, ūnxī	*anoint, smear*
20	ūnus, ūna, ūnum	*one*
	urbānus, urbāna, urbānum	*fashionable, sophisticated*
5	urbs, urbis, f.	*city*
	urna, urnae, f.	*bucket, jar, jug*
	ursa, ursae, f.	*bear*
	ut	*as*
10	uxor, uxōris, f.	*wife*

V

7	valdē	*very much, very*
11	valē	*good-bye*
	valvae, valvārum, f.pl.	*doors*
	varius, varia, varium	*different*
10	vehementer	*violently, loudly*
	vehō, vehere, vēxī	*carry*
	vēnātiō, vēnātiōnis, f.	*hunt*
6	vēndō, vēndere, vēndidī	*sell*
	venia, veniae, f.	*mercy, forgiveness*
5	veniō, venīre, vēnī	*come*
	vēr, vēris, n.	*spring*
11	verberō, verberāre, verberāvī	*strike, beat*
	verrō, verrere	*sweep*
	versus, versūs, m.	*verse, line of poetry*
	versus magicus, versūs magicī, m.	*magic spell*
16	vertō, vertere, vertī	*turn*
	sē vertere	*turn around*
	vērus, vēra, vērum	*true, real*
19	vexō, vexāre, vexāvī	*annoy*
1	via, viae, f.	*street*
	vibrō, vibrāre, vibrāvī	*wave, brandish*
	vīcī *see* vincō	
	vīcīnus, vīcīna, vīcīnum	*neighboring, nearby*
	victima, victimae, f.	*victim*
	victor, victōris, m.	*victor, winner*
3	videō, vidēre, vīdī	*see*
20	vīgintī	*twenty*
	vīlicus, vīlicī, m.	*farm manager, overseer*
	vīlis, vīlis, vīle	*cheap*

	vīlla, vīllae, f.	*villa, (large) house*
15	vincō, vincere, vīcī	*win, be victorious*
	vindex, vindicis, m.	*champion, defender*
	vindicō, vindicāre, vindicāvī	*avenge*
3	vīnum, vīnī, n.	*wine*
11	vir, virī, m.	*man*
	virga, virgae, f.	*rod, stick*
	vīs, f.	*force, violence*
13	vīs *see* volō	
	vīsitō, vīsitāre, vīsitāvī	*visit*
13	vīta, vītae, f.	*life*
	vītō, vītāre, vītāvī	*avoid*
	vitreārius, vitreāriī, m.	*glassmaker*
	vitreus, vitrea, vitreum	*glass, made of glass*
	vitrum, vitrī, n.	*glass*
6	vituperō, vituperāre, vituperāvī	*find fault with, tell off, curse*
19	vīvō, vīvere, vīxī	*live, be alive*
19	vix	*hardly, scarcely, with difficulty*
	vōbīs *see* vōs	
4	vocō, vocāre, vocāvī	*call*
13	volō, velle, voluī	*want*
	quid vīs?	*what do you want?*
10	vōs	*you (plural)*
19	vōx, vōcis, f.	*voice*
	vulnerātus, vulnerāta, vulnerātum	*wounded*
13	vulnerō, vulnerāre, vulnerāvī	*wound, injure*
20	vulnus, vulneris, n.	*wound*
13	vult *see* volō	

Index of cultural topics

Index of grammatical topics

Time chart

Date	Alexandria and Britain	Rome and Italy
BC *c.* 2500	Salisbury Plain inhabited	
c. 2200–1300	Stonehenge built	
c. 1900	Tin first used in Britain	
c. 1450	Wessex invaded from Europe	
c. 900	Celts move into Britain	
c. 750	Plow introduced into Britain	Rome founded (traditional date) 753
post 500	Maiden Castle, Iron Age fort in Britain	Kings expelled and Republic begins, 509
		Duodecim Tabulae, 450
4th C	Hill forts used by Celts	Gauls capture Rome, 390
331	Alexandria founded	
311–285	Ptolemy Soter, first Greek ruler in Egypt	Rome controls Italy/Punic Wars, 300–200
280	Ptolemy II builds Pharos	Hannibal crosses the Alps, 218
c. 250	Septuagint (translation of Bible), Alexandria	Rome expands outside Italy, 200–100
post 240	Eratosthenes, scientist/librarian	Gracchi and agrarian reforms, 133–123
		Cicero, Roman orator (106–43)
55–54	Julius Caesar invades Britain	
48–47	Julius Caesar in Alexandria	Julius Caesar assassinated, 44
41–42	Mark Antony and Cleopatra in Alexandria	Augustus becomes emperor, 27
31	Egypt becomes a Roman province	Virgil, author of the *Aeneid*, 70–19
13	Obelisks re-erected before Caesareum	
AD 1st C	Alexandrians use monsoon pattern to India	Tiberius becomes emperor, 14
60	Boudica leads Iceni revolt	Nero emperor, 54–68
		Great Fire at Rome/Christians blamed, 64
		Vespasian emperor, 69–79
c. 75	Fishbourne Palace begun	Colosseum begun, *c.* 72
78–84	Agricola governor in Britain	Titus emperor, 79–81
c. 80	Salvius arrives in Britain	Vesuvius erupts, 79
2nd C	Galen studies in Alexandria	Tacitus, historian, *c.* 56–117
		Domitian emperor, 81–96
c. 200		Trajan emperor, 98–117
296	Origen, Christian scholar in Alexandria	Hadrian emperor, 117–138
328	Diocletian besieges Alexandria	Septimius Severus dies in Britain, 211
391	Athanasius, bishop in Alexandria	Constantine tolerates Christianity, 313
c. 400	Serapeum and Daughter Library destroyed	Bible translated into Latin, *c.* 385
410	Hypatia, woman philosopher in Alexandria	Alaric the Goth sacks Rome, 410
	Rome refuses Britain help against Saxons	Last Roman emperor deposed, 476

World history	World culture	Date
Babylonian/Sumerian civilizations		BC c. 3000
Pharaohs in Egypt		c. 3000–332
Indo-European migrations, c. 2100	Maize cultivation, American SW	c. 2000
Hammurabi's Legal Code, c. 1750	Epic of Gilgamesh	post 2000
Minoan civilization at its height, c. 1500	Rig-Veda verses (Hinduism) collected	c. 1500
Israelite exodus from Egypt, c. 1250	Development of Hinduism	c. 1450
Israel and Judah split, c. 922	Phoenician alphabet adapted by Greeks	c. 1000–800
Kush/Meroe kingdom expands	Iliad and Odyssey	c. 800
	First Olympic Games	776
Solon, Athenian lawgiver, 594	Buddha	c. 563–483
	Confucius	551–479
Persia invades Egypt and Greece, c. 525–400	Golden Age of Greece	500–400
	Death of Socrates	399
Conquests of Alexander the Great		335–323
	Museum founded in Alexandria	290
Great Wall of China built		c. 221
Judas Maccabaeus regains Jerusalem	Feast of Hanukkah inaugurated	165
	Adena Serpent Mound, Ohio	2nd C
		106–43
Julius Caesar in Gaul, 58–49	Canal locks exist in China	50
	Glassblowing begins in Sidon	post 50
Cleopatra commits suicide		30
Herod rebuilds the Temple, Jerusalem		c. 20
Roman boundary at Danube, 15	Birth of Jesus	c. 4
	Crucifixion of Jesus	AD c. 29
Britain becomes a Roman province, 43	St Peter in Rome	42–67
	St Paul's missionary journeys	45–67
	Camel introduced into the Sahara	1st C
		64
Sack of Jerusalem and the Temple		70
Roman control extends to Scotland		77–85
	Paper invented in China	c. 100
		c. 56–117
	Construction at Teotihuacán begins	c. 100
Roman empire at its greatest extent		98–117
Hadrian's Wall in Britain		122–127
"High Kings" of Ireland		c. 200–1022
Byzantium renamed Constantinople, 330	Golden Age of Guptan civilization, India	c. 320–540
	Last ancient Olympic Games	393
Mayan civilization		c. 300–1200
Byzantine empire expands		518

Date	Alexandria and Britain	Rome and Italy
? 537	Death of King Arthur	Gregory the Great, pope, 590–604
9th–10th C	Saxon forts against the Vikings	Period of turmoil in Italy, 800–1100
c. 900	Alfred drives Danes from England	Republic of St Mark, Venice, 850
973	Cairo replaces Alexandria as capital	
1189–1199	Richard the Lionheart	
12th C	Robin Hood legends circulated	Independent government in Rome, 1143–1455
1258	Salisbury Cathedral finished	Marco Polo travels to the East, 1271–1295
1346	Battle of Crecy, cannon first used	Dante, poet, 1265–1321
1348	Black Death begins	Renaissance begins in Italy, *c.* 1400
1485	Henry VII, first Tudor king	Botticelli, painter, 1445–1510
1509–1547	Henry VIII	
1517	Ottomans conquer Egypt	Titian, painter, 1489–1576
		Rebuilding of St Peter's begins, 1506
		Michelangelo starts Sistine Chapel ceiling, 1508
1558–1603	Elizabeth I	Rome sacked by German/Spanish troops, 1527
1577–1580	Drake circumnavigates the globe	Spain controls much of Italy, 1530–1796
1588	Defeat of Spanish Armada	
1603	James I, first Stuart king	
1649	Charles I executed	Galileo invents the telescope, 1610
1649–1659	Cromwellian Protectorate	Bernini, architect and sculptor, 1598–1680
1660	Restoration of Charles II	
1675	Wren begins St Paul's Cathedral	
1760–1820	George III	
1789	Wilberforce moves to end slave trade	
1795–1821	John Keats, poet	
1796	Smallpox vaccination in England	Napoleon enters Italy, 1796
1798	Napoleon invades Alexandria	Verdi, composer, 1813–1901
1798	Nelson defeats French at the Nile	
1807	Muhammad Ali develops Alexandria	
1833	Factory Act limits child labor in Britain	Mazzini, Garibaldi, Cavour, active 1846–1861
1837–1901	Victoria, queen	Victor Emmanuel II, united Italy, 1861
1844	Railways begin in Britain	
1863–1933	Cavafy, Alexandrian poet	
1869	Suez Canal opened	
1882	British occupation of Egypt	Marconi invents wireless telegraphy, 1896
1911	N. Mafouz born, Nobel winner	
1924	Egypt declares independence	Mussolini controls Italy, 1922–1945
1940	Churchill Prime Minister	
1944	Arab League starts in Alexandria	Italy a republic, 1946

World history	World culture	Date
	Birth of Muhammad	570
Charlemagne crowned, 800	Arabs adopt Indian numerals	*c.* 771
Vikings reach America, *c.* 1000	*1001 Nights* collected in Iraq	ante 942
Norman invasion of England, 1066	*Tale of Genji*, Japan	1010
First Crusade, 1096	Ife-Benin art, Nigeria	1100–1600
Magna Carta, 1215	Classic Pueblo Cliff dwellings	1050–1300
Genghis Khan, 1162–1227	Al-Idrisi, Arab geographer	1100–1166
Mali empire expands, 1235	Arabs use black (gun) powder in a gun	1304
Joan of Arc dies, 1431	Chaucer's *Canterbury Tales*	ante 1400
Inca empire expands, 1438	Gutenberg Bible printed	1456
Turks capture Constantinople, 1453	Building at Zimbabwe	*c.* 15th C–*c.* 1750
Moors driven from Spain, 1492	Vasco da Gama sails to India	1497–1498
Columbus arrives in America, 1492		
	Martin Luther writes *95 Theses*	1517
Cortez conquers Mexico		1519–1522
Mogul dynasty established	Magellan names Pacific Ocean	1520
French settlements in Canada, 1534	Copernicus publishes heliocentric theory	1543
	Shakespeare	1564–1616
Burmese empire at a peak	Muskets first used in Japan	*c.* 1580
Continuing Dutch activity in the East	Cervantes publishes *Don Quixote*	1605
Pilgrims land at Plymouth Rock, 1620	Taj Mahal begun	1632
Manchu dynasty, China, 1644–1912	Palace of Versailles begun	1661
Peter the Great rules Russia, 1682–1725	Newton discovers the Law of Gravity	1682
	J. S. Bach, composer	1685–1750
Industrial Revolution begins, *c.* 1760	Mozart, composer, 1756–1791	*c.* 1760
US Declaration of Independence	Quakers refuse to own slaves	1776
French Revolution begins	Washington, US President	1789
Napoleon defeated at Waterloo	Bolivar continues struggle, S. America	1815
Mexico becomes a republic, 1824	S. B. Anthony, women's rights advocate	1820–1906
American Civil War, 1861–1865	Communist manifesto	1848
Lincoln's Emancipation Proclamation		1863
Canada becomes a Dominion	French Impressionism begins	1867
Serfdom abolished in Russia, 1861	Mahatma Gandhi	1869–1948
Cetewayo, king of the Zulus, 1872	Edison invents phonograph	1877
	First modern Olympic Games	1896
First World War, 1914–1918	Model T Ford constructed	1909
Bolshevik Revolution in Russia, 1918	Bohr theory of the atom	1913
	US Constitution gives women the vote	1920
Second World War		1939–1945
United Nations Charter		1945